HAUNTED CANADA

The Second Terrifying Collection

Joel A. Sutherland

illustrations by
Norman Lanting

Scholastic Canada Ltd
Toronto New York London Auckland Sydney
Mexico City New Delhi Hong Kong Buenos Aires

For Colleen.
I owe every page in this collection to you.

Scholastic Canada Ltd.
604 King Street West, Toronto, Ontario M5V 1E1, Canada

Scholastic Inc.
557 Broadway, New York, NY 10012, USA

Scholastic Australia Pty Limited
PO Box 579, Gosford, NSW 2250, Australia

Scholastic New Zealand Limited
Private Bag 94407, Botany, Manukau 2163, New Zealand

Scholastic Children's Books
Euston House, 24 Eversholt Street, London NW1 1DB, UK

www.scholastic.ca

Library and Archives Canada Cataloguing in Publication

Title: Haunted Canada : the second terrifying collection / Joel A.
Sutherland ; illustrations by Norman Lanting.

Other titles: Works. Selections

Names: Sutherland, Joel A., 1980- author. | Lanting, Norman, illustrator.
| Container of (work): Sutherland, Joel A., 1980- Haunted Canada 4. |
Container of (work): Sutherland, Joel A., 1980- Haunted Canada 5. |
Container of (work): Sutherland, Joel A., 1980- Haunted Canada 6.

Description: A collection of three previously published works.

Identifiers: Canadiana 20190069147 | ISBN 9781443175197 (softcover)

Subjects: LCSH: Ghosts—Canada—Juvenile literature. | LCSH: Haunted
places—Canada—Juvenile literature.

Classification: LCC BF1472.C3 S97 2019 | DDC j133.10971—dc23

6 5 4 3 2 1   Printed in Canada   139   19 20 21 22 23

MIX
Paper from
responsible sources
FSC® C103567

INTRODUCTION

It's been more than six years since I started working on *Haunted Canada 4*, the first volume I wrote in this series that was begun by author Pat Hancock. A lot has changed since then, but one thing that hasn't changed is my love of a good ghost story.

Picture yourself sitting around a campfire with your family, or in a dark basement with some sleepover friends, or on your family room couch with your siblings after a late night spent trick-or-treating. Someone asks, "Do you want to hear a story?" What sort of story do you suppose they're about to tell? And are you excited? Or growing a little nervous?

If you're like me, you're hoping they're about to tell a scary story, and you're both excited and nervous. That's what makes tales of things that go bump in the night so much fun — you want to know what happens next while simultaneously dreading what happens next. You want to close your eyes and cover your ears but you don't want to miss a single gory detail.

If anything, my love of ghost stories has increased since I began writing this series. Remember, the stories in this collection are all true. Yes, that's right; they really happened to people. And speaking to so many who claim to have experienced paranormal encounters while researching the haunted history of infamous locations across the country has made me even more fascinated in ghosts than ever before. But believe me when I tell you that these tales still wreak havoc on my nerves, and I have no doubt they'll do the same to you.

So, dear reader, do you want to hear a story?

Frightfully yours,

HORROR CINEMA VERITÉ

Coquitlam, British Columbia

The sound of footsteps on the second floor when you're alone in the house, an unfinished basement's locked trap door rattling on its hinges, a ghastly wail in the middle of the night — if you're a fan of scary movies, you're familiar with these cinematic clichés. Maybe you don't even jump when a shrieking cat leaps out of a dark corner, or when someone — or *something* — passes in front of the camera, unseen by the clueless characters on screen.

But for one actor with a small role in a horror movie filmed in an abandoned mental hospital, the biggest scares happened off-camera, and they weren't special effects. They were all too real. Riverview Hospital is home to a host of evil spirits that have plagued film crews working in the building for years. One of those spirits is particularly vicious. It has razor-sharp teeth, a wicked bite and can run incredibly fast on all fours. Big dogs can be terrifying, but coming face to face with a *dead dog*? The horror movie actor will tell you that's much, much worse.

To understand where the negative energy within the abandoned mental hospital comes from, we need to go back to its beginning. In 1904 the province of British Columbia had a problem. The Provincial Asylum for the Insane in New Westminster was seriously overcrowded. With more than three hundred patients, children were forced to live side by side with potentially dangerous psychiatric patients. Reports started to surface of inadequate care, terrible hygiene and horrendous living conditions. A new, bigger building was needed, and it was needed right away.

The province purchased one thousand acres of land in 1904 and, in 1913, the Hospital for the Mind (later called Riverview Hospital) opened its doors in Coquitlam. It was considered to be on the cutting edge of psychiatric hospitals, but it wasn't long before the cracks started to appear — figuratively and literally. Electroshock therapy was used in an attempt to cure patients of their "insanity," as well as the highly controversial psychosurgery, or lobotomy, wherein a small piece of the brain is surgically removed. By 1951 there were nearly five thousand patients in Riverview Hospital, and serious overcrowding was once again a major concern.

The problem slowly corrected itself as the medical field shifted from favouring large mental hospitals to smaller buildings with fewer patients, and the population of Riverview gradually dwindled. In July 2012 it closed its doors for good.

Over the years the foreboding grandeur and general creepiness of the old buildings have made Riverview a beacon for film production companies. Many horror movies and television shows have been filmed in Riverview's dusty halls, making it the most filmed location in Canada.

But with such a powerful and long history of grief and pain etched into the hospital's walls, the scariest events have sometimes happened after the cameras stopped rolling.

Film crews working through the night have reported seeing former patients and staff suddenly appear and disappear. People have been shoved by unseen forces. The tunnels in the basement are said to be so full of negative energy that it's nearly impossible to enter them.

In 2004 an actor named Caz, quite possibly bored and most certainly brave, spent his nights exploring Riverview when he wasn't needed on set. The horror movie was being filmed in the West Lawn Building, which had been closed for more than twenty years.

In the infamous basement tunnels, he felt like he was being watched and sensed a bad presence. However, it was the fourth floor that turned Caz into a firm believer in ghosts.

It was after midnight. Caz stood alone at the end of a hallway that ran the length of the building. It was pitch-black other than the dim red light from an EXIT sign. He waited, rooted to the ground because he sensed . . . something.

Suddenly a dog charged at him from the far end of the hall. It was impossibly fast. And as it neared him, Caz noticed the beast was transparent. It lunged at him but, just before its teeth tore into his legs, the dog disappeared.

Caz didn't believe his own eyes, so he returned two

more nights to see what would happen. Each night the phantom dog charged him, and each night it disappeared moments before knocking him down. Perhaps the phantom dog is charged with protecting the "Lady Bug Room," the fourth floor room where the majority of Riverview's paranormal activity takes place. The room received its unusual nickname in part because of the unexplained red dots, believed to be spirits, that often appear near the room in photographs.

The Lady Bug Room is odd, to say the least. Its door is the only one on the fourth floor that's locked. It's also the only door without a doorknob, making it impossible to enter. Finally, it's the only room in an otherwise uninhabited and powerless building with light streaming through the crack beneath the door.

What's inside the Lady Bug Room? No one really knows, but it's rumoured that an evil presence known as "The Candy Lady" dwells within. One thing known is that the fourth floor was at one time where the lobotomies were performed.

Caz couldn't resist the morbid desire to see what was in the Lady Bug Room. He returned one night and peered in through the keyhole. He pressed his ear against the door. He slowed his breathing and strained to hear something, anything. The hall became unnaturally quiet. And then he heard it, the sound from within the locked room in the abandoned mental hospital that sent him running as fast as his legs could carry him.

The sound of someone breathing.

Horror movies don't hold a candle to the real-life horrors found at the end of darkened hallways, in musty tunnels and behind locked doors.

The West Lawn Building, Riverview Hospital

ROTTING IN A CAGE

Lévis, Quebec

"There is scarcely any woman in all of Canadian history who has a worse reputation than Marie-Josephte Corriveau." So reads the opening sentence of Corriveau's entry in the *Dictionary of Canadian Biography*. In life, Marie-Josephte Corriveau was a beautiful woman, but in death she became something vile and heinous, a sickening reminder to the people of Lévis to obey the letter of the law.

Born in Saint-Vallier, Quebec, in 1733, she married her first husband, a farmer named Charles Bouchard, at the young age of sixteen. They had three children and remained together for eleven years despite whispered rumours that theirs was not a happy, peaceful union. The townsfolk believed that Charles was mean and abusive to his young wife. Marie-Josephte was miserable, and many thought she might be better off on her own. Nevertheless, no one suspected the woman of any wrongdoing when Charles was found dead in 1760, nor did it seem strange that Marie-Josephte should remarry a mere fifteen months later. The times were tough and she had to put the well-being of her children first, assuring they'd have a roof over their heads and food to eat.

She married another farmer, Louis Etienne Dodier. All seemed well at first, but it wasn't long before cracks began to appear in their relationship and it would soon come to a deadly end. A mere year and a half after the wedding, Louis was found dead in his own stable. Marie-Josephte argued that their horse must have kicked and trampled her new husband — his head was caved in and his face covered in lacerations — but the locals were no longer so trusting of the young woman. An inquiry was launched by the British military authorities who had recently conquered New France. It was quickly ruled that the horse played no part in Louis's death.

It was well known that Marie-Josephte's father, Joseph, did not approve of his daughter's second marriage and was on bad terms with Louis. The military tribunal found him guilty of the homicide and sentenced him to hang, while Marie-Josephte was found to be an accomplice and sentenced to sixty lashes and to be branded with the letter M on her hand.

Neither punishment was carried out. On the eve of his execution, Joseph finally admitted that he had wanted to protect his daughter from the hangman's noose and therefore hadn't proclaimed his own innocence, but in reality he had played no part in Louis's death. The guilt, he confessed with a heavy heart, lay entirely upon his daughter's shoulders.

7

A second trial began and Marie-Josephte testified to striking her husband twice on the head with an axe while he slept. She then dragged his body from the house to the horse stable to make the murder look like an accident. No one knows why she decided at this time to admit the truth. Perhaps her guilty conscience was too much to bear. Perhaps, like many serial killers, she craved attention. But with the admission of guilt came new speculation about the mysterious and sudden death of her first husband. And her legend has grown over the years to falsely claim she had as many as seven husbands, all of whom she murdered in gruesome fashions such as poisoning, strangulation and impalement with a pitchfork. It's even been said she boiled one of her husbands alive.

The charges against Joseph Corriveau were dropped and Marie-Josephte was sentenced to hang for her crimes. But that punishment alone would not be satisfactory for such an evil and treacherous person who some were now coming to believe was a sorceress with dark powers. After hanging, her corpse was ordered to be placed in an iron cage in the shape of a human body and strung up for public display.

The terrible act was carried out in 1763. Her cadaver was hung in the cage at a busy crossroads in the woods that would later become known as La Corriveau Forest. The cage — body and all — was left swaying in the wind for thirty-eight days to serve as a warning. Her skin blackened and peeled away from her bones. Her hair fell out, and animals picked at her flesh. The stench was atrocious. But as her body withered away, so did the belief that Marie-Josephte could no longer harm the living.

The eerie sounds of grinding metal and clattering bones kept most late-night travellers from venturing near the cursed intersection. Those who weren't superstitious or easily spooked, and passed the swaying cage, arrived at their destinations with pale faces and stories of the rotting body that had opened its eyes, lunged for them with decaying hands and whispered their name with a guttural voice. With every passing day, the stories grew wilder and more frightening. Marie-Josephte's body was finally moved to a nearby cemetery, but no one was brave enough to free it. Cage and Corriveau were buried together.

The townsfolk had hoped that'd be the last they'd hear of Marie-Josephte, but they were dead wrong. Not long after she had been buried, an upstanding young man named François Dubé was travelling home to his wife. When he passed the tree where the cage used to hang, he saw an odd vision across the river. Demonic figures danced wildly around the crackling flames of a blue fire. Just as François turned to flee, a pair of bony, slimy hands clutched his throat from behind and held him in place.

"Take me across the river, Dubé," the rotting corpse of Marie-Josephte hissed in his ear. "I cannot pass the blessed waters of the Saint Lawrence unless a Christian man carries me."

François fell to the ground as he tried to free himself from Marie-Josephte's supernaturally strong grasp. As he pulled at her arms, her maggot-ridden flesh ripped off her bones and wriggled in his hands. François finally succumbed to extreme fright and fainted in a heap on the side of the road. His wife found him there the next morning, nearly paralyzed with fear but thankful to still be alive.

Reports of the ghost of Marie-Josephte rising from her grave to torment passersby in La Corriveau Forest still creep up today. Those who remember her tale — and it's nearly impossible to forget — are wise to get off the roads, out of the woods and into the safety of their homes long before nightfall in the city of Lévis.

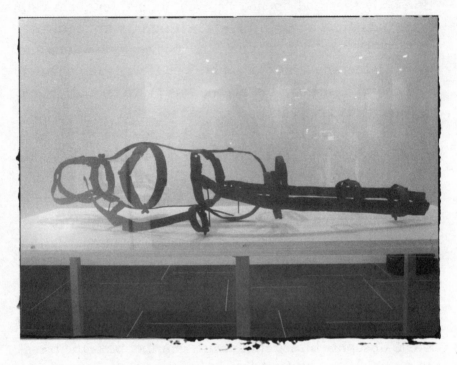

The cage that held Marie-Josephte Corriveau's body

RED EYES IN THE NIGHT

Roche Percée, Saskatchewan

Some ghosts are peaceful, others are mean-spirited. But regardless of their disposition, most seem unable to do much physical harm to the living. That couldn't be further from the truth when it comes to the rugeroos that haunt the abandoned Roche Percée mines. According to legends that date back hundreds of years, rugeroos are spirits with red eyes that cut through the dark. They are monstrously huge and can appear as a mix of man and animal, most commonly the coyote. And they guard their territory fiercely, attacking anyone who dares to venture too close.

Roche Percée is a small village southeast of the city of Estevan. Translated from French its name means "pierced rock," which describes the odd geological formation. The village grew in the 1880s when people discovered coal, which was dug out of the ground and transported to Winnipeg. The first large-scale coal mine was established in 1891. Within a few years there were dozens of mines in operation, and Roche Percée was a bustling community of miners and fortune-seekers. But by the 1950s most of the coal-mining companies had left, and in 2011 a massive flood forced many of the remaining residents to abandon their homes, leaving behind a ghost town of damaged buildings and empty mines.

The pierced rock also remains, a massive landmark of sandstone that juts up from the ground like a giant, bony hand from a grave. The wind blowing through its many holes, tunnels and crevices creates an eerie screech that has long been revered and feared by all who hear it. Those who are brave enough to enter the tunnels have felt compelled to inscribe their names on the rock walls,

Postcard of Roche Percée dated 1917

including General Custer and his famed U.S. 7th Cavalry in the 1800s.

Rugeroo sightings have been reported by tourists and locals for as long as Roche Percée has existed. The only sound they make is a low, menacing growl. And, if their target doesn't flee immediately, they attack. Those who are wise enough to retreat are followed by the spirit's disembodied red eyes through the woods far from the rugeroo's territory.

Reports of these spirits have varied, but each description is as terrifying as the last. Courtney Chistensen was once stalked by a rugeroo. It was a fat, furry creature, taller than a deer, part wolf and part bear. Jan Drummond described a rugeroo that was spotted walking on the roof of a school. It had the head and antlers of a deer and the legs of a man. Everyone swore that seeing it was a bad omen.

So if the sight of a giant half-man, half-beast ghost with glowing red eyes wasn't enough to send you running, now you know that it's also a bad omen — just in case you might've otherwise decided to stick around when a rugeroo confronts you in the woods.

THE HANGED MAN

Bridgetown, Nova Scotia

"The Prettiest Little Town in Nova Scotia" — that's the unofficial motto of Bridgetown (population 949), which was incorporated in 1897. Victorian houses line the streets, the small-town shops are huddled close together and people greet each other warmly on every street corner. An annual triathlon in the summer and a cider festival in the fall draw happy crowds. It's quiet and peaceful, and that's exactly how the townsfolk like it.

But then the townsfolk aren't the ones spending their evenings at the Stem ta Stern Bed and Breakfast. They aren't the ones who have discovered Bridgetown nights can be anything but quiet and peaceful. They aren't the ones huddled under their bedsheets, listening to the hollow *rat-a-tat-tat* of bony fingers upon their windows.

The Stem ta Stern is a Queen Anne revival home with two guest rooms. Much of its period architecture has been preserved, including the stained glass, the front turret and the original wood throughout. Bridgetown was once a vital shipbuilding town with plenty of wealth, and the beautiful homes reflect this heritage. They also have the perfect look for a movie about a haunted house and, in the case of the Stem ta Stern, the perfect ghost.

One week after purchasing the property, the owner was awoken with a start by an odd sound she assumed was caused by the wind. She slipped out of bed and went down the stairs to make sure all was well and to get a drink of water. She passed a storage room. She paused. The air drifting under the door was unnaturally cold. And then she heard a sound that chilled her to the bone. *Rat-a-tat-tat, rat-a-tat-tat.* It sounded like someone was tapping on a window, and it appeared to be coming from inside the storage room.

She opened the door and entered the room. What she saw outside the window immediately caught her attention. There was a man hanging by his neck from a large tree, swaying in the wind. She jumped in alarm, but when she looked out the window again, the dead man had disappeared.

It's suspected the man had committed suicide, but no one knows who he was or what exactly happened to him. That doesn't stop the man from frightening guests from time to time. The reports are always the same. Late at night, the bedroom's temperature plummets for no apparent reason. Someone issues a warning on the window: *rat-a-tat-tat, rat-a-tat-tat.* But then, instead of hanging from the tree outside, the man suddenly appears in the hall or a room. His face is distorted with pain and his neck is twisted and bruised. It's a terrifying vision that forces guests to scream and shut their eyes tight, and when the guest finally finds the courage to open his or her eyes again, the hanged man is gone.

If the reports from the Stem ta Stern are to be believed, it would appear the prettiest little town in Nova Scotia harbours a secret that's neither pretty nor little.

THE TOMBS OF HELL

Kingston, Ontario

Throughout the year, in fair weather or foul, Kingston tourists are led along shadowy streets and through dark alleys, soaking up every gruesome detail that's shared during one of the country's oldest haunted walks. The tour guides, clad in black robes and carrying a burning lamp, love to chill their groups to the bone with terrifying true stories. But although it's the job of the guides to get under the groups' skin, one ghost is simply too evil, too malicious, to mention.

The ghost is that of George Hewell, a Kingston Penitentiary inmate who was shot to death by the chief keeper in 1897. Hewell was, by all accounts, a particularly bad seed in a jail filled with the worst criminals our country has ever known. He was so bad, in fact, that not even death could stop him from tormenting the guards and his fellow inmates.

Before it closed in 2013, Kingston Pen was the most infamous prison in Canada. It was home to such notorious criminals as Clifford Olson, Paul Bernardo and Russell Williams. Opened in 1835, Kingston Pen predates Confederation and has been designated a national historic site. After 178 years it was deemed to be in a rundown state and too costly to continue operating. The inmates were moved to other jails, but the stories of the terrible things that took place within its imposing limestone walls live on.

In the early days, one form of punishment was to tie a prisoner to a post to be flogged up to forty times with a cat-o'-nine-tails, a nasty whip designed to inflict as much pain and damage on someone's back as possible. Others were disciplined by being branded with a hot iron that burned the flesh, forever marking them as criminals. And there was no shortage of hangings on the premises. Back then an illegal act as mild as stealing a cow or forging a receipt was punishable by death.

Much of this barbaric behaviour was carried out by the first two wardens, father and son Henry and Frank Smith. Henry designed what he called "the box," a wooden coffin that forced inmates to stand upright with no space to move a muscle. Prisoners were left in the box for nearly ten hours and were poked and jabbed by guards through the air holes. Frank allegedly enjoyed shooting at prisoners with a bow and arrow, sticking them with pins and needles as if they were human pincushions and forcibly pouring salt into their mouths.

Although the treatment of prisoners improved over the years, the dark energy created by so much hate and suffering has remained, forever soaked into the stone walls. Some have said entering Kingston Pen is akin to being forced into the tombs of Hell.

Is it the ghost of George Hewell people sense upon walking into the prison? His vengeful spirit has been spotted before. A front page article titled "Did They See a Ghost?" in the *Kingston Daily News* on February 13, 1897, described an eerie encounter with Hewell, who had been dead a year by that time.

With moonlight reflecting brightly off freshly fallen snow, two guards on night duty rounded a corner in the outside courtyard and saw a man in convict's clothing step through the hospital door. The man, described as a "nocturnal visitor" who had a "strange form," silently crossed the courtyard without paying the guards any attention. They ordered him to identify himself and explain what he

Kingston Penitentiary

was doing out so late, but the man turned and walked back to the hospital door without a word. The guards levelled their rifles to shoot and gave him one last warning. The man turned to face them, touched the hospital door and suddenly disappeared before the guards' disbelieving eyes. They later admitted that they both had immediately recognized the shadowy figure as George Hewell. A late-night search of the prison failed to resolve the mystery.

Before his death, Hewell had been serving a life sentence in Kingston Pen. He had a reputation for attacking anyone within his reach, including guards and fellow inmates. There were at least four recorded incidents in which he tried to kill other convicts, and his murderous instincts could be set off for the most insignificant reasons. He once tried to kill a man for borrowing his library book. He was like a box of dynamite ready to explode at any moment.

The story surrounding Hewell's death is both gruesome and riveting. Early one morning he tried to throw another convict over a three-storey balcony to his death. As punishment he was confined in an isolation cell for some time and then forced to work for the rest of the day in the tailor's shop. This was a mistake, as it gave Hewell, angered and irrational, access to a pair of sharp tailor's shears.

With the shears concealed on his body, Hewell swore and caused a commotion from within his cell through the rest of the evening. After listening to the racket for as long as they could, the guards entered the cell to move Hewell to another location where he could be further punished. Hewell seized his opportunity and attacked the guards with the shears. Fortunately for the guards, he wasn't able to seriously injure anyone before the warden pulled his pistol's trigger and lodged a bullet in Hewell's head.

Normally, a bullet to the head would be enough to kill any man, but Hewell was no regular man. For five full hours Hewell continued to swear and threaten the guards before finally succumbing to the head wound.

With his final breath, Hewell levelled a curse at Kingston Pen. He promised to return from beyond the grave to make everyone pay for killing him — even those who played no part in his death. Dying wouldn't stop him from having his revenge.

Many eerie occurrences since the guards' moonlit patrol have been attributed to the vengeful spirit of Hewell, a man who was never at peace. When he first arrived at Kingston Pen and passed through the front gate of the tombs of Hell, Hewell knew he was serving a life sentence. But he couldn't have known he'd also be serving an after-life sentence.

REBECCA'S CONCRETE GRAVE

Moncton, New Brunswick

There's a slab of concrete on the side of the rarely travelled Gorge Road in northern Moncton. On the surface
there's nothing entirely remarkable about the concrete
— it appears as if it might have been poured there quite
by mistake many years ago and forgotten. A ramshackle
fence surrounds the slab, protecting it from farm equipment or snowplows. But the locals know what lies beneath
it. Perhaps the only reason the story isn't well known
outside New Brunswick is because they'd rather keep the
truth as deeply buried as the bones below the concrete at
the side of the road.

In 1876, farm girl Rebecca Lutes was sixteen years old.
Her family had been lured to southeastern New Brunswick
from America with a land grant from the British. There was

no shortage of farmable land in Canada, just a shortage of farmers. Many people emigrated from the States, Ireland, Holland, Germany and other far-flung countries to work the land and produce desperately needed crops. Many of the immigrants brought their superstitious beliefs with them to Canada. Misfortune, bad weather, illness — these could all be attributed to evil forces.

The summer of 1876 had been especially dry, providing little food in the fields and leaving Moncton susceptible to flash fires. A few families lost their barns and homes to raging forest fires, which only made the food shortage worse. As fall turned to winter, a new problem arose: farmers throughout the area were waking in the morning to find that their livestock had disappeared overnight. The community was desperate to find something — or rather, someone — to blame.

Compounding the situation were reports of bizarre lights floating along the roads after dusk and rumours of demonic rituals being practised deep in the woods. The townsfolk, at their wits' end, agreed that there must be a witch among them.

The story isn't clear on how they came to believe Rebecca was the guilty party, but it was said that she had been seen practising witchcraft and had stolen the animals herself, using their blood for sacrificial purposes in her dark ceremonies. She was tried, found guilty and sentenced to death.

One heartbreaking version of the tale claims that Rebecca was hanged from a tree on her own property as her family was forced to watch. Her body was then cut down and buried at the base of the tree. But the townsfolk feared a dead witch almost as much as a live one, so they took extreme precautions with the burial.

First, her body wasn't placed face up as is customary, but face down. This was to prevent the witch from digging her way back up to the surface should she return from the dead. Instead she'd dig her way straight down to Hell. Second, they poured a four-block concrete casing into the hole to further prevent her from rising from her grave.

Despite their best efforts to seal her six feet under for eternity, the locals began seeing Rebecca wandering the fields at night, and these reports continue today. Sometimes Rebecca takes the form of a thick, misty cloud, and other times people see floating orbs of light that are attributed to her. The land around her concrete grave is often unnaturally cold. People have seen their breath on muggy summer days and car windows have frozen over as vehicles pass her resting spot. Fresh bloodstains often appear on the surface of the concrete grave only to fade away moments later. There's an old abandoned church across the street, and Rebecca has been spotted peering down at the living from an upper window. But she hasn't always been spotted alone; many have seen a black cat sitting on the concrete, both during the day and at night. When approached, the cat suddenly disappears. Some people believe the phantom feline is waiting for the day when Rebecca returns to this plain permanently.

The concrete grave remains on the side of Gorge Road to this day. Visiting it after midnight has become a rite of passage for local teenagers. It's a story so spine-chillingly compelling that it can't remain a secret from the rest of the country for long.

THE FAMILY THAT HAUNTS TOGETHER

Colwood, British Columbia

For most young cadets training for a life in the military, the people they fear the most are their superiors. This wasn't the case at Hatley Castle, a mansion located on the grounds of what was once Royal Roads Military College, a naval training facility from the 1940s to 1995.

Who could be more frightening than a drill sergeant barking orders and demanding push-ups? The family who built and lived in Hatley Castle, that's who. The family who died many years before the military college opened. The family reunited in the afterlife and none too pleased with the new tenants of their beautiful home.

James Dunsmuir was at one time the most influential and wealthy man in the entire province of British Columbia. He was born while his father (who would become a Vancouver Island coal baron) and mother emigrated from Scotland to B.C. in 1851. He stepped out of his father's shadow to become a powerful industrialist and politician, holding the positions of both Premier and Lieutenant-Governor of British Columbia in close succession. The mansion Dunsmuir built in 1908 for his large family, Hatley Castle, was designed in the Scottish baronial style, reflecting his heritage.

"Money doesn't matter. Just build what I want," he reportedly told the contractors. Dunsmuir, his wife, Laura, and their children (they had twelve, nine of whom survived infancy) loved their home. It's not hard to understand why.

The mansion boasted fifty rooms on 640 acres that also had farms, a modern dairy and its own slaughterhouse. A fishing lodge was built on property along the Cowichan River. The gardens were so extensive and magnificent that Dunsmuir had to employ one hundred gardeners and groundskeepers. It was the type of home that would be hard to leave behind. For the Dunsmuirs, the act of packing up and moving on would prove impossible, even in death.

Despite the luxury in which he lived, James Dunsmuir's final days were not happy. One of his two sons had died in 1915 when the RMS *Lusitania* sank and the other, an alcoholic, had left home to roam the world aimlessly, tarnishing the family's name. And Dunsmuir's daughters had married and moved far away, leading lives that Dunsmuir believed to be frivolous. He died in his fishing lodge in 1920. At the time of his death, he was still the richest man in the province, but in a few short years his entire fortune had been squandered by his children. Hatley Castle was sold to the government in 1940. The years between Dunsmuir's death and the selling of Hatley Castle were harder on no one more than Dunsmuir's widow, Laura. She had become accustomed to the elegant life she had enjoyed, entertaining celebrities and the British aristocracy in her home. She fell into depression, grew very ill and passed away in 1937.

Soon after her death, a maid reported feeling terribly uncomfortable while working alone in the house. She couldn't shake the feeling that someone was watching her as she worked, and there were some rooms that she couldn't bring herself to enter.

When Hatley Castle became Royal Roads Military College in 1941, the tales of peculiar incidents began to increase. Cadets were often overcome by a discomforting sensation in the middle of the night, as if they had suddenly stepped into an ice-cold spider web. And imagine waking to see an old woman staring down at you before vanishing into the night? Many cadets have experienced just that, and their descriptions of the old ghost perfectly match Laura Dunsmuir. They say she didn't look happy to see so many young men living in her house. One night, she decided to take matters into her own hands.

A cadet who was acting as senior duty officer fell asleep but was awoken suddenly a few hours later when someone pulled his leg. He sat bolt upright and blinked in the darkness, expecting the culprit to be one of his superiors or a fellow cadet, but he couldn't believe his eyes: it was the ghost of Mrs. Dunsmuir, hell-bent on dragging him out of his bed and out of her house. He tried to free his leg but, despite his strength and Mrs. Dunsmuir's small stature, the spectre held onto him with an unearthly ferocity. Finally the young cadet was able to shake himself free from her cold, dead hands, and Laura Dunsmuir dissipated in the air before him. When the cadet shared his experience the next morning, he discovered he wasn't alone — many other cadets had also been attacked and pulled from their beds by the deceased widow.

Although Mrs. Dunsmuir is the angriest ghost that haunts Hatley Castle, she's not alone. James Dunsmuir has been seen floating through the basement walls, surrounded by bright white light, and some of their children have also been spotted. The property has now become a university, and the students enrolled there often report ghostly run-ins with the Dunsmuirs. The family that haunts together, sticks together, even beyond the grave. The students and professors can only hope that James Dunsmuir and his children don't become as violent as Laura Dunsmuir has proven herself to be.

Hatley Castle

HOSPITAL OF THE DEAD

Inglewood, Alberta

A bloody handprint smeared on a door, dried-up blood caked on every surface in a room and bugs crawling everywhere. These are the horrific sights that confronted an anonymous young thrill-seeker who snuck into the Charles Camsell Hospital in Inglewood late one night with her older brother and his friends. The flashlights gripped in their trembling hands did little to brighten the ghostly atmosphere of the abandoned hospital. After describing the bloody scene above, the girl could say no more, simply concluding that there are things in the creepy building that you don't want to see. She still has nightmares about it.

She isn't the only one to warn against venturing into the abandoned hospital. Others have reported that the floors and walls on the second floor, which used to be the hospital's surgical ward, are covered in old bloodstains. Take a trip up to the fourth floor and you're now standing in what used to be the hospital's psych ward. Stay a while and chances are good you'll hear soft screams slowly getting louder and closer. If you somehow manage to stand your ground, a teenage girl who was once a patient will slowly creep out of the shadows. Look closely at her hands and you'll see why she's still screaming years after her death: before she died many years ago, she ripped each of her own fingernails free from her fingertips.

Confronted by such a ghastly image, it's safe to say no one would be able to resist the urge to flee, but it's best to take the stairs (even though barbed wire has been wrapped around the handrails in an attempt to keep people out). The elevators to the morgue occasionally travel up and down on their own, as if the spirits of all the bodies once kept there can't stay put in the basement.

What makes Charles Camsell Hospital such a magnet for paranormal activity? Although it was a place that helped many people get better over the years, there are also a few dark and troubling secrets etched into its history.

Between the years of 1945 and 1967 it was an experimental hospital offering an occupational therapy program for Indigenous patients. Shock treatment was administered without consent and there were isolation rooms where terrified patients were locked in the dark on their own. It is widely suspected that the staff not only abused the Indigenous population, but also murdered some of the patients. If that's not upsetting enough, it's also rumoured that there's an unmarked mass grave of Indigenous children near what used to be the staff garden.

It's no surprise that stories of vengeful spirits at the

Charles Camsell Hospital continue to surface. Most recently, a man who was contracted to clean part of the building one night with a few co-workers shared his story. The phones, left behind and not used in more than twenty years, rang repeatedly while they worked through the night. When the cleaners picked up the ringing phones, there was no dial tone — the lines were dead. In one of the rooms, the cleaners saw the outline of a small child suddenly form on a dust-covered chair. When they entered the basement — the old morgue — they all had trouble breathing, and a deep, bloody cut suddenly appeared on the back of a woman's hand.

Charles Camsell Hospital

That was enough to send them running from the building. They jumped in their vehicle and sped away, leaving the Charles Camsell Hospital looming on the horizon behind them.

But for as long as the hospital could be seen in their rear-view mirror, the team leader's cell phone rang and rang and rang. When he finally mustered the courage to look at his phone's screen, it read:

1 missed call: The Charles Camsell Hospital

DUEL TO THE DEATH

St. John's, Newfoundland and Labrador

There was a time, not too long ago, that the honourable way for two gentlemen to settle a serious dispute was to stand back to back, walk ten paces, turn . . . and fire pistols at each other. Instead of firearms, others preferred to brandish steel. Regardless of the method, these so called "honourable" duels often ended in bloodshed, death and sometimes, historic hauntings.

The last duel to be held on Canadian soil took place in St. John's in 1873, but it wasn't fatal for either duellist. Another St. John's duel in 1826, however, did end in death — a death so unnecessary and tragic that the loser couldn't bring himself to leave this plain.

Sipping rum toddies and huddled around a blazing fireplace during a bitter Newfoundland night, the officers of the British army and Royal Veteran Company stationed at Fort Townshend passed their time by gambling at cards. Among those present were Captain Mark Rudkin and Ensign John Philpot, and as cold as it was outside, the tension between these two was heated. Not only were they adversaries in the card game of lansquenet being played, but they were also competing for the affections of the Irish daughter of a St. John's businessman who lived in Quidi Vidi Village. This rivalry had already caused Philpot, the younger of the two men, to insult Rudkin at a public event, an occurrence for which he had later begrudgingly apologized. On the night of the card game, there was certainly no love lost between the two military men, and the presence of alcohol and gambling did nothing to decrease their contempt for one another.

Philpot was on a losing streak, while fortune smiled upon Rudkin. The other men in the game folded their hands and gradually bowed out until only Philpot, still losing, and Rudkin, still winning, remained. Philpot was desperate to end on a winning note to recoup some of his losses, and the pot had grown to nearly three pounds, quite a large sum in those days. Rudkin dealt the final hand, and his own happened to be the winning one.

It couldn't be so. Philpot was sure of it. Rudkin, out of his dislike for Philpot, must have cheated. Philpot accused Rudkin of rigging the final hand and tried to grab the money. Rudkin scoffed, denied the charge, and made for the door with his winnings. Enraged, drunk and blinded by his hatred for Rudkin, Philpot threw a glass of water in his face.

Rudkin, to his credit, kept his cool and tried to diffuse the situation, but Philpot wouldn't let it go and continued to goad the captain. With the other officers playing witness and his honour and reputation at stake, Rudkin challenged Philpot to a duel. Philpot agreed without reservation.

Early the next morning, March 30, the two men met a mile outside of town near Brine's Tavern at Robinson's Hill. Rudkin had once again cooled down and offered to call off the duel. Philpot, however, was still fuming and insisted that Rudkin must have cheated. He refused the captain's offer.

With loaded pistols, they stood back to back, walked apart ten paces and turned. Philpot fired first. Luckily for Rudkin the shot just grazed his collar. Now, with time on his side and the perfect opportunity to shoot Philpot, Rudkin took the higher road. He raised his pistol above his head and fired his shot into the air. The duel had ended without bloodshed.

Anyone else in Philpot's position would consider himself fortunate to still be breathing, but Philpot saw it as a second opportunity to rid the world of Rudkin. He insisted that a second round take place despite the fact that such an act wasn't customary. (Traditionally, if the opponents of a duel survived the first round, both would retain their honour and the dispute was considered to be resolved.) With no other option, Rudkin had to accept the challenge. But this time he did not purposely fire his shot wide. His bullet found a home in Philpot's chest, buried deep in his right lung. The ensign flew backwards and died not long after he hit the ground, a victim of his own stupidity and stubbornness. He was buried, coincidentally, on April Fool's Day.

Rudkin was charged with murder and a short trial followed. Public sympathy was initially on Philpot's side, but it quickly shifted to Rudkin's as the full story — with

Rudkin's many attempts to save the young ensign — came to light. On April 17, Rudkin was carried from the court-house on the shoulders of his friends and supporters after being found not guilty, but disturbing reports began to surface from Robinson's Hill, the location of the duel.

Rudkin's horse had become skittish as he rode to the duel on that chilly March morning, as if the animal could sense the tragedy that lay ahead. Others have reported the same odd behaviour from their horses near the spot where Philpot's blood soaked the ground. Some have come face to face with Philpot's ghost and noticed a bloody hole on the chest of his military uniform. It's been said that he wanders the streets at night near the place where he died, still angry and eternally longing for a rematch. After all, he was not only "cheated" in his pursuit of love, the card game and the duel, but when Rudkin was found to be innocent of murder, Philpot was cheated out of his post-humous justice as well. Some grudges carry on beyond the grave.

THE MOB PRINCESS

Fort Saskatchewan, Alberta

Many male convicts were hanged years ago at the North West Mounted Police outpost in Fort Saskatchewan, but only one woman. In 1923 Florence Lassandro, a woman dubbed the "Mob Princess," was executed for a crime she may or may not have committed. She was only twenty-two years old.

In fact Florence was the only woman ever to be hanged in the province of Alberta. She was born Florence Costanzo in Italy and moved to the Canadian province with her family when she was a young girl. At fifteen years of age, she was still a young girl when she married Charles Lassandro.

Charles worked for a businessman named Emilio Picariello who, among other things, owned an ice cream company and the Alberta Hotel. But his legitimate businesses were merely a front for a successful bootlegging operation he had started. Emilio made a lot of money sneaking booze from Alberta, where it could be purchased legally, into the state of Montana during the early part of the nineteenth century.

Charles introduced his wife to the mob boss Emilio, which set her down a dark path. Florence earned the name Mob Princess by working her way up within Emilio's criminal organization and performing smuggling runs herself. It's possible Florence, who never seemed too fond of her husband, was actually in love with Emilio's son, Steve, who was also a player in his father's bootlegging business.

In 1921 Steve Picariello was shot by Alberta Provincial Police Constable Steve Lawson during a high-speed chase. Wounded, Steve Picariello managed to escape to British Columbia. Upon hearing that his son had been shot, and believing him dead, Emilio teamed up with Florence and tracked down Constable Lawson. They confronted him in front of his house. An argument broke out and Lawson was fatally shot in the back. The horrific scene played out before the mortified eyes of Lawson's nine-year-old daughter, Pearl.

Emilio and Florence were both convicted of the murder, although Florence proclaimed until her last day that she was innocent and that it was Emilio who had shot Constable Lawson. Despite the fact that there was no conclusive proof of who shot the constable, the jury found both Emilio and Florence guilty of the crime. The Mob Princess was hanged on May 2, 1923, at the Fort Saskatchewan jail before a small group of witnesses hand-picked by the hangman.

But did she truly leave her life behind, or was hers a story steeped too heavily in crime, bloodshed and unrequited love to ever leave this world?

The Fort Saskatchewan Museum & Historic Site now sits on the land where Florence was hanged. It's a picturesque historic village with eight heritage buildings (including the warden's house and a portion of the jail) decorated with period furniture. Visitors walking the grounds get a sense of what life was like in the bygone era, and schoolchildren enjoy field trips to the Museum & Historic Site throughout the year. But if you stay past sundown, you might experience a "bygone" event you wish you could forget.

There have been many reports of lights turning on and off, objects moving on their own and faces seen in windows. A clairvoyant and medium visited the grounds and picked up on many unexplained cold spots, thick atmospheres and spiritual energy in the buildings. One woman who used to work at the museum suddenly quit because of the ghost haunting the area.

Even Curator Kris Nygren, who calls herself a skeptic, has to admit that those who have seen eerie things on the property are "believable" people and reliable sources. And Darlene Briere is perhaps the most believable and reliable of all. Darlene conducts research for the museum and volunteers for special events and programs. One Halloween Darlene was involved with Fright Night, a special children's sleepover on the grounds. While taking a late-night walk between the blacksmith's shop and the jail, she saw an odd mist take shape in the moonlit woods and snapped a couple of pictures. When Darlene examined one of the photos, she saw the clear image of a young woman's face within the fog. It was, she strongly believes, the face of Florence.

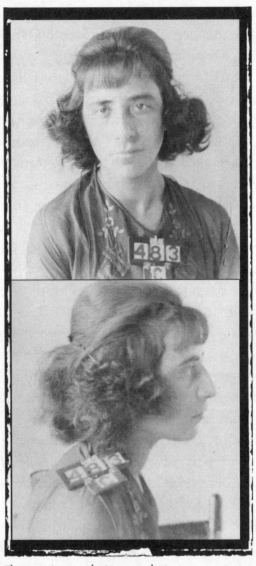

Florence Lessandro's mug shots

Later that night, while making sure all the young guests were safe in their beds, she entered an empty building and saw a curtain moving, as if a person was hiding behind it. Suddenly, the curtain fell to the floor in a heap. Darlene lifted the curtain with trembling fingers and there, for the briefest of moments, she saw the face again.

If you dare to visit the location of the Mob Princess's execution, so could you.

THE MAN IN GREY

Saskatoon, Saskatchewan

Upon entering the Delta Bessborough Hotel in downtown Saskatoon, you might want to keep your eyes on your feet. There's a large crack in the marble floor of the main lobby. You wouldn't want to trip on the spot where a man fell to his death many years ago.

The Bessborough — or "Bess" as it's affectionately called — was completed in 1932 but didn't open to the public for three years due to the economic hardships of the Great Depression. Designed to resemble a Bavarian fortress, it's well known for its imposing facade and castle-like appearance. It's also well known for the crack in the floor and the ghost of the man who might have created it with his head.

There's no shortage of people who have seen an elderly

gentleman walking through the banquet level late at night. The reports are always the same: he's tall, slender and well dressed in a grey suit and fedora, a popular fashion during the 1930s. "The Man in Grey," as he's called, is always pleasant, smiles at passersby and will occasionally offer a quiet hello, but is otherwise silent. When guests mention the oddly attired but nice old man they passed in the hall, employees of the Bess chuckle and inform the guests that they've just been greeted by a ghost.

That's perhaps the most striking thing about The Man in Grey. Guests and employees alike are amazed by how lifelike he appears, unlike other ghosts who are transparent or bear the injuries that claimed their lives.

One question lingers in the air like smoke from a snuffed candle: Did The Man in Grey crack the marble floor? Bess employees seem to think so. They share a story about an employee — a nice old man from the 1930s who dressed impeccably — who was sent upstairs late one night to deal with noise complaints. There was a party in one of the rooms that was disturbing the other guests on the same floor. The employee knocked on the door and kindly asked if the revellers could keep the noise down. The men answered his request with an insane action rather than words. Two men picked up the employee and threw him over the balcony. He fell seven storeys to his death, cracking his skull and the floor below. Current-day Bess employees think the ghost belongs to this kind and unfortunate man who was simply doing his job.

Colin Tranborg, founder of Paranormal Saskatchewan, saw The Man in Grey late one evening and has also heard a compelling first-hand account from a group of ghost hunters. They snuck into a storage closet on the hotel's top floor and saw a man staring at them from outside through

The Delta Bessborough Hotel

a window. Terrified, they wondered how he wasn't falling to his death — there was simply no way to explain it. Unless he'd already fallen to his death back in the 1930s.

There are other ghosts staying at the Bess. Guests have reported running into a disturbed woman in one of the upper floors' hallways. She screams bloody murder when approached and then suddenly disappears. And the spirits of two small children are thought to live in one of the stairwells, playing together for all eternity.

But there's no doubt The Man in Grey is the Bess's most famous ghost, perhaps because he's such a happy soul. People seem more inclined to speak about him than the other spirits. After all, if you came face to face with a ghost in the dead of night, wouldn't you rather be greeted with a "hello" than a ghastly shriek?

THE SHOW MUST GO ON AND ON AND ON

Dawson City, Yukon

The Yukon Territory is a mysterious and wild land. During the weeks before and after the winter solstice, the capital city, Whitehorse, has only five and a half hours of sunlight per day. It's the promised land for things that go bump in the night, giving ghosts with an aversion to daylight free reign to roam the pitch-black streets for more than eighteen hours a day. And the Klondike Gold Rush of the late nineteenth century left a string of abandoned outposts — many still perfectly preserved today — that are ghost towns in more than name alone.

Dawson City, with a population of about one thousand, is far from a ghost town, but it's also a far cry from the forty thousand people who lived there in 1898. The gold rush kicked off in 1896 when three men found gold in Bonanza Creek. Within two years Dawson City was filled with miners looking to stake their claim and entrepreneurs hoping to cash in on the population boom. But the Yukon was a dangerous land, and mining was dangerous work. Many people lost their lives during the gold rush, often in brutal fashion, and it was common to bury the corpses in unmarked graves. It's believed that an undercurrent of supernatural energy hums through the city's bones to this day on account of the bloodshed and tragedies that occurred during the gold rush, and one ghost takes centre stage in Dawson City. It's a ghost that appears to be aflame. A ghost of one of the city's most famous previous residents.

But the ghost doesn't belong to popular writers Pierre Berton or Jack London, both of whom once called Dawson City home. Nor is it the ghost of any of the Dawson City Nuggets, a hockey team that travelled to our nation's capital in 1905 by ship, train and dogsled to lose the most lopsided series in Stanley Cup history to the Ottawa Silver Seven. The flaming ghost is that of Kathleen Rockwell, better known as Klondike Kate.

As a young girl, Kate was a free spirit and a tomboy, more comfortable playing with boys than girls and frustrated by the lack of opportunities for women in the late 1800s. Her temper was as fiery as her bright red hair, and her rebellious nature kept her from settling in one spot for long. She was expelled from school before trying, unsuccessfully, to break into show business in New York City. In 1899, hearing of the gold rush and envisioning the influx of miners to Dawson City desperate for entertainment, she travelled to the Yukon. However, Kate was refused entry by the Royal Canadian Mounted Police, who were trying to control the number of people rushing into the territory.

Never one to be intimidated by authority nor hindered by rules, Kate is reputed to have disguised herself as a boy and hidden upon a boat that had gained clearance to travel from Alaska to the Yukon.

Not long after arriving in Dawson City, Kate joined the Savoy Theatrical Company and began performing in daily shows at the Palace Grand Theatre. Her notoriety and fame sparked as quickly as a match, thanks in large part to her signature "flame dance." She spun many yards of red chiffon around her body to create the illusion that she was on fire in the middle of the stage, and it wasn't long before everyone knew Klondike Kate. Other nicknames followed, such as the Darling of Dawson. And, thanks in no small part to her, Dawson City became known as the Paris of the North.

Dawson City's new reputation for being an entertainment centre was also created by the work of struggling bartender Alexander Pantages, who became a theatre owner and eventually a movie mogul. Kate and Pantages grew very close and it seemed like her star would never fall nor lose its shine, but their relationship was as turbulent as a Yukon winter storm. Pantages left Kate at the same time the gold rush came to a screeching halt.

After a few years of mining, it had become apparent that there wasn't as much gold in the area as everyone had hoped. Dawson City saw its population plummet as quickly as it had risen. The forty thousand people who lived there in 1898 all but disappeared overnight, leaving only eight thousand residents by 1899 and 615 by 1911. Dawson City was no longer a city, and although the Palace Grand Theatre remained, Klondike Kate was left without an audience. She eventually packed up and left town. After another string of unsuccessful attempts to find her footing in show business, she ended her days playing the part of a social outcast and recluse. She died on February 21, 1957.

But the show must go on. Although she died in America, it's said that Kate's spirit returned to the beloved location of her glory days, the Palace Grand Theatre in Dawson City. Her ghost is believed to haunt her old dressing room and people have reported seeing a blazing red swirl in the middle of the stage during the night when no one else is in the theatre. Bronwyn Jones was a stage manager of the Palace Grand from 2002 to 2004, and she believes the intensely short time frame of the Klondike Gold Rush — and the amount of history that happened in such a short span — might be part of the reason for the spiritual energy that's still felt in the building's walls.

Dawson City is now a major tourist attraction, drawing sixty thousand visitors each year. The Palace Grand Theatre still puts on performances, many of which reflect life in the Old West. And then, once everyone has left after the final show of the evening, Klondike Kate takes the stage and performs her fire dance for an audience of none.

Klondike Kate

THE SHADOW IN YOUR BEDROOM

Iqaluit, Nunavut

With extremely bitter winters and very short summers, the city of Iqaluit, capital of Nunavut, is too cold to grow trees. Amongst the snow, ice and rock you'll only find hardened, scraggly bushes. Winter temperatures average -30°C to -45°C. The howling Arctic winds chill to the bone and exposed skin can freeze in minutes, but a shadowy man who watches people while they sleep has been even more effective at turning people's blood to ice.

There used to be a townhouse complex in Iqaluit called White Row that many former tenants believed to be haunted. The entire complex tragically burned to the ground in 2012 in a blaze that the city's fire chief deemed to be suspicious.

Bumps in the night, knocking on the walls and phantom

footsteps in the halls were common bedtime sounds in White Row. Most people brushed the odd noises off as the sounds of an old building or rationalized that they must've been caused by the winter wind, but others saw what — or rather, *who* — was the source of the disturbances within White Row.

There was a man, a shadowy man — a shadowy man who watched people at night. Most often it was young children and teenagers who saw the shadowy man. Imagine: one moment you're alone, the next moment you see the shadowy man in your doorway, and the moment after that he's gone. He never made a sound or moved a muscle, and he seemed incapable of passing through doors or entering rooms. It appeared as if his sole purpose was to stare at the living after they'd gone to bed.

One young girl reported seeing the shadowy man for the first time shortly after her family moved into White Row. He appeared in her doorway while she was alone and freaked her out so much that she ran straight to her sister's room. One night, as the girl was talking to her cousin, she spotted the shadowy man in her closet out of the corner of her eye, staring out from the darkness within. He appeared in her room every single night until the family moved into a new home.

Despite her initial fear, the girl said she grew accustomed to the shadowy man and learned to live with the unexplained phenomena. He didn't give off an evil energy, she said, although his appearances were often preceded by an unusual feeling. The girl even began to believe that the shadowy man was there to protect her.

Everyone who saw the shadowy man described him as tall and pale, but his most disconcerting characteristic was his neck. A deep purple bruise ringed it, as did the deep outline of a rope. It was believed he used to live in White Row and committed suicide somewhere in the building, trapping his soul within. Whether he was unable to pass through doorways or voluntarily chose not to (and even if he was there to protect the people he watched), his presence certainly didn't make it easy to fall asleep at night.

A shadow passing by a bedroom door or the sound of something stirring in the darkness of a closet might simply be products of imagination . . . but then again, it might be something else, something unexplainable.

Something real.

HAUNTED NIGHTMARES

Selkirk, Manitoba

Like many infamously haunted locations, St. Andrew's on the Red attracts a regular procession of ghost hunters. People have seen chilling sights and heard unnatural sounds, but most distressingly, many have suffered from a recurring nightmare that keeps them up all night for weeks following their visit. A nightmare of an unseen presence rattling the cemetery gates so viciously that it threatens to tear them off their hinges.

Built between 1845 and 1849, St. Andrew's on the Red in Selkirk (twenty-two kilometres northeast of Winnipeg) is the oldest stone church in Western Canada. Its small cemetery is filled with locals that succumbed to plagues such as influenza, diphtheria, typhoid and tuberculosis, as well as many notable people who played a role in

Manitoba's history. It's little wonder that it's also a hot spot for paranormal sightings.

When the Hudson's Bay Company and the North West Company amalgamated in the 1820s, many workers either retired or lost their jobs. Some of these people settled with their families in what is now Selkirk along the Red River. Archdeacon William Cockran built a wooden church in 1831, the outline of which can still be found directly behind the present stone church. When you set foot inside this holy place, you're immediately struck by the history within, as much of the interior has remained unchanged since 1849.

Old, gnarled trees cast shadows on the cemetery grounds. You'll find the crumbling tombstones of Archdeacon Cockran; E.H.G.G. Hay, first leader of Manitoba's Official Opposition Party in 1870; Alexander Christie, Chief Factor of the Hudson's Bay Company; and Captain William Kennedy, an Arctic explorer who searched for Sir John Franklin's lost expedition in 1851. Stick around after nightfall and this quiet, peaceful burial place becomes decidedly less so.

There are spine-tingling reports from late-night church-goers who have seen a man in black and a woman in white drifting a foot above the cemetery's ground. Rumour has it that the woman died during the church's construction and sometimes appears on the balcony during services. Others have seen a ghost car appear out of thin air and pull up to the cemetery's gate. It sits and idles for a moment — perhaps looking to pick someone up or to drop someone (recently deceased, most likely) off — before disappearing. The strangest regular sighting in the St. Andrew's on the Red cemetery is a pair of red eyes peering out from behind tombstones and trees, silently watching

St. Andrew's on the Red

those who walk the grounds at night.

While enrolled in the Creative Communications program at Red River College, Jenn Twardowski and a classmate filmed the cemetery for a school project. Even under the safety and comfort of daylight they had a disconcerting experience. They were followed by a weird, unexplainable noise similar to a hammer striking a nail in a coffin. Both of the students were simultaneously relieved and creeped out when they learned the other had heard the spooky sound as well.

Although Jenn set out to capture one of the spirits on film, she should count her blessings that she did not. Those who have seen the man in black, the woman in white, the phantom car or the red eyes have all suffered from hideous nightmares. These night terrors are filled with the violent rattling of the church's gates. Some believe the nightmares are a plea for help from the church's ghosts. Others see them as a dark omen and a dire warning never to return.

DEAD-EYED DOLLS

Ottawa, Ontario

The Bytown Museum couldn't have a more picturesque location in our nation's capital. Housed in the oldest stone building in Ottawa, the museum is on the lower locks of the Rideau Canal at the Ottawa River, nestled in the heart of downtown between Parliament Hill and the Chateau Laurier Hotel.

But the petite museum's beauty and charm are in direct contrast with the truly terrifying experiences that visitors and employees have reported. In fact, it's considered by many paranormal experts to be the most haunted location in the entire country. Something lives in the museum's displays, skulking through the artifacts and taking possession of the antique dolls that sit in silent rows, watching everyone who wanders up to the second floor unawares.

57

The building was constructed in 1827 by the British military as a supply storehouse and treasury during the construction of the Rideau Canal. Death was always hanging over the building in those early years, as nearly one thousand workers died in gruesome construction accidents and from diseases such as malaria. Undeterred by the tragic deaths of so many workers, the military continued work on the canal under the leadership of Lieutenant Colonel John By in order to defend against invasion from the United States. Although Lt. Col. By died in 1836, some believe his ghost still lingers by the still waters of the Rideau Canal.

Today the Bytown Museum houses a permanent collection of artifacts celebrating Ottawa's history, and it's not uncommon for visitors to be overcome by an uneasy feeling while they're observing the displays. On the second floor is a collection of antique dolls that has caused some of the greatest unease. If it's very quiet and you're all alone, close your eyes and strain your ears. You might hear the faint sounds of a child crying. Open your eyes and you might even catch one of the dolls winking at you as if you're in on some ghastly joke. Those who have heard the crying and seen the blinking eyes believe the spooky porcelain dolls are possessed by the spirits of dead children.

Other visitors have said they have been pushed, grabbed or tripped from behind when alone, typically in the creepy old money vault and the stairwell. Some museum-goers have heard an angry, bodiless voice shout, "Get out! Get out!" But the majority of the paranormal reports come from the museum staff, and the most hair-raising activity tends to occur after the public has left for the night.

One employee noticed a man sitting in the library after she had closed up. She asked him to leave, and he obliged without a word, silently walking to the door. A second after he stepped outside, she realized she hadn't seen the man enter the museum while they were open — an impossibility in such a small, intimate building — so she flung the door open to ask how he had gotten in. Although it had only been a brief moment since the man had left and she could see a far distance in every direction, the man had completely vanished.

Glen Shackleton, chairman of the board of directors, has no doubt the Bytown Museum is haunted, and he has a couple of chilling stories to back up this claim. One night he and three others were the only four people in the building. They closed a sliding door and it immediately began to vibrate violently as if someone on the other side was hitting it. A review of the security camera footage showed that no one was there, but as soon as the assault on the door ended they heard heavy footsteps walking away. The late-night encounter with an unseen presence was enough to send Glen's three companions running from the museum.

Glen believes, as many others do, that the ghost who causes these disturbances is Duncan McNab. Duncan was a supply manager during the construction of the Rideau Canal. But Glen also thinks there might be at least one other prominent ghost within the walls of the museum, someone who had a much larger role in the canal's construction.

Another night he was having a casual chat with a museum employee about the ghost of McNab when the woman's computer inexplicably turned off. A moment later it turned itself back on, but her normal desktop didn't appear. Instead, the monitor was blank other than the words "Lt. Col. John By" repeated over and over on the screen. It was as if the colonel himself was listening in on the conversation and wanted to make it clear that McNab's ghost isn't the only spirit haunting the Bytown Museum. Nor does it seem that either man is ready to leave his life's work behind.

THE BLOODY BATTLEFIELD

Quebec City, Quebec

Although it only lasted a mere fifteen minutes, the Battle of the Plains of Abraham was one of the bloodiest in Canada's history. It's said the lawns grow so lush and green today thanks to the litres of French and British blood that were spilled there on September 13, 1759. It's estimated that more than 1,300 soldiers were killed or injured during the battle. That's roughly three people every two seconds. With so much life lost in such a violent way and in such a short period of time, it's little wonder Battlefields Park, named in commemoration of the historic battle, is widely considered to be the most haunted location in Quebec.

The Battle of the Plains of Abraham was fought on a plateau just outside the walls of Quebec City on land that was owned by a farmer named Abraham (which explains the battle's name). Although it was over quickly, it was the culmination of a three-month siege by the British and was a pivotal moment in Canadian history. It's interesting to ponder how Canada, known as New France at the time, would be different today if the British had lost the battle and hadn't taken control of Quebec from the French.

That's not to say that the British didn't suffer during the battle. Far from it. The two sides had nearly an identical number of casualties and wounded soldiers, and both leaders, British General James Wolfe and French Lieutenant General Louis-Joseph de Montcalm, died from wounds suffered on the battlefield. Moreover, they both welcomed death as if the Grim Reaper were an old friend.

Wolfe was struck in the stomach and chest by two shots near the beginning of the battle and fell to the ground. Upon hearing a soldier shout, "They run, see how they run," Wolfe opened his eyes and asked who was running. When he heard the French lines had broken and they were fleeing, he sighed in relief and said, "Now, God be praised, I will die in peace." These were his final words. He died immediately after uttering them.

During the retreat, Montcalm was struck repeatedly in his lower abdomen and thigh. He managed to escape but died from the wounds early the next morning. When he was informed by the surgeons trying to save his life that his wounds were mortal, he calmly replied, "I am glad of it." The surgeons added that he didn't have long to live. "So much the better," Montcalm said gravely. "I am happy that I shall not live to see the surrender of Quebec." His body was buried in a crater created by an exploded bombshell, a grim location of his own choosing.

Battlefields Park's concealed location and many hidden

nooks and crannies have made it notorious for illicit activities such as duels, muggings and even executions. These dastardly doings have given the park a dark reputation. It's believed that the most dangerous time to visit is September — not because of an increase in criminal activity, but an increase in *paranormal* activity.

General James Wolfe

Lieutenant General Louis-Joseph de Montcalm

On cold nights in September, especially near the thirteenth and the anniversary of the battle that took place in 1759, the spirits of the fallen soldiers rise from the once blood-soaked ground to re-enact the warfare. People have smelled sulfur hanging heavily in the air and have heard cannons firing. Pallid-looking ghosts in eighteenth-century uniforms have been seen wandering the plain and rushing to and from the entrances to the tunnels beneath the park.

Is it possible that General Wolfe and Lieutenant General Montcalm, two men who weren't afraid of death, rise from their graves to lead their spectral armies into battle on the anniversary of their battle? Go for a daytime stroll through Battlefields Park and take a good look at the grass beneath your feet. It is unnaturally green, particularly after September 13. Could it be that it's not mere fertilizer that makes each blade so vivid and bright?

GHOST TOWN TUNNELS

Tranquille, British Columbia

Fifteen minutes west of downtown Kamloops, British Columbia, in a scenic valley surrounded by water and trees and mountains, is a ghost town known as Tranquille. More than forty buildings have sat idle for years. Long ago they fell into disrepair and their boarded up doors and shattered windows have given the town a creepy, unwelcoming face. Even under the comfort of the midday sun, it's easy to picture the many ghosts that have been seen here over the years. But if you enter one of the abandoned Tranquille buildings, the ghosts who dwell within might not be behind your back but *below your feet*.

The town notorious for hauntings gets its ironic name from the Tranquille River, which flows into Kamloops Lake. In 1907 the Tranquille Sanatorium was built to treat people diagnosed with tuberculosis (or TB). TB was a widespread epidemic in the early 1900s and the sanatorium filled with patients so quickly that an entire town blossomed around it. There were homes, dormitories, a schoolhouse, a cafeteria, a gymnasium, a fire hall, a large laundromat, a cemetery . . . even farms and their own steam plant, making the town completely self-sustained. This was designed to minimize the town's need to be in contact with the outside world. Simply put, people came to Tranquille to die.

According to official records, nearly 1,600 people, mostly children, died of TB in Tranquille. In order to move the bodies between buildings without creating a commotion or disturbing the other patients, nearly two kilometres of tunnels were built beneath Tranquille's streets. While townsfolk went about their business above ground, the dearly departed went about theirs below ground.

After the Tranquille Sanatorium closed in the 1950s, the property changed hands a few times (becoming a hospital to treat the mentally ill, and an ill-fated amusement park, of all things). In 1983 the property was completely abandoned and the buildings began to fall into disrepair. Tranquille became a desolate place, haunted by the tragic memories of what had transpired there, and this, of course, attracted a new interest in the area. Curiosity seekers, ghost hunters and teens looking for a place to spook each other snuck into the town after nightfall. Many were too afraid of the unsettling vibe in the air to ever leave their cars, but those who were brave enough were treated to a truly eerie experience. At one time the sanatorium was filled with rusting wheelchairs and dirty medical equipment, and the operating room was painted with old bloodstains. One woman who worked there when it was a mental hospital said all the staff and patients regularly heard screams in empty wards and shuffling in unoccupied beds, and these sounds still reverberate through the building today. Rumour has it that a nurse was murdered by a patient long ago, leaving her spirit to forever wander the grounds.

But the most frightening place on the property remains the dark tunnels that snake their way through the dirt below the town. People have heard voices and seen shadowy figures in these murky depths, as if the ghosts of the bodies that were once carted underground are still stuck six feet under.

Staff of Tranquille Farm — the new owners — recently made an unusual discovery during an investigation of the tunnels: near the morgue where the bodies were stored are a dining hall and a barbershop, giving new meaning to the expression "a hair-raising experience."

In Tranquille, you get two ghost towns for the price of one — one above ground, one below. Few have the guts to venture very deep into either, let alone both.

A GHOSTLY ALMA MATER

St. Thomas, Ontario

As mortified onlookers watched in horror and recorded the event on their mobile phones, the towering and iconic steeple of Alma College collapsed a little after noon on May 28, 2008. The grand, Gothic building had been engulfed in a raging inferno, the fire started by two teenage boys. Fortunately, no one was harmed in the fire as the college had sat vacant since it closed in 1988. But one has to wonder what became of the tormented souls that haunted the building after the blaze reduced it to cinders and ash.

The most well-known ghost of Alma College haunted its halls for nearly a century. It was an all-girls private school built in 1878 that focused its studies on literature, art and music, with a student body that included young women from around the globe.

Elissa Lyman, a student from 1983 to 1986, lived nearby and therefore didn't sleep in the dormitory like so many of her classmates. She recalls with unease the times when winter weather made it too dangerous to drive home after class, forcing her to spend the night. They were often restless, those nights spent in the dorm, as her sleep was plagued by the bizarre sounds that filled the school. The only explanation Elissa could think of for the midnight noises was that they were caused by the wanderings of Angela, the spirit the girls dubbed "the Ghost of Alma" in hushed tones.

The details surrounding Angela are a little hazy and stories vary, but a retired teacher confirmed that the faculty and staff reported seeing her ghost in the castle-like building as early as the 1930s. Most people believe that Angela was a music teacher, although some assert she was a house mother (someone assigned to ensure the young girls behaved appropriately and patrolled the halls after curfew). Regardless of Angela's position within Alma College, everyone agrees that she was a mean woman who was nasty toward the students, making her disliked by all.

Legend has it a group of teen girls decided to play a prank on Angela, hoping to give her a taste of her own medicine. They locked her in a cupboard and left her there overnight, but it's unlikely they intended for their "joke" to have such dire consequences. The cupboard was too small and sealed airtight, and Angela soon ran out of air. Her suffocated body was found the next morning.

Shortly thereafter, her ghost was seen in what was nicknamed the Ivory Tower, one of two stairwells leading to a storage room on the second floor at the south end of the building. Some have reported that if you stay alone in the Ivory Tower long enough you'll see her descending the stairs, and others not brave enough to attempt that feat have heard her footsteps walk past. It's a telling sign that the Ivory Tower's walls were unmarked while the second tower's walls were covered with the signatures of generations of schoolgirls. Apparently, no one wanted to deface the stairwell where Angela dwelt.

Many years after Alma College closed and began to fall into disrepair, a team of ghost hunters snuck onto the grounds and crept through the dust-covered halls. They slowly climbed the creaking stairs to the very top of the Ivory Tower. Here, one of the braver people in the group knocked on the wall. It was answered by the hollow sound of another knock.

"Is this Angela?" the ghost hunter asked.

"Yes," said a very low whisper.

As this was the very type of experience the group had hoped for, they didn't turn and run. They also noted that, despite Angela's reputation for having gone through life as a mean-spirited woman, her ghost did not give them a bad vibe. Perhaps she has remained on this plane to atone for her sins and to make up for the way she mistreated her young students. Perhaps she's a new woman, so to speak.

The peaceful feeling the group got from Angela, however, did not extend to the rest of the college. They constantly felt unwanted and surrounded by a dark, evil energy that they attributed to many ghosts, some old but most young. At first the spirits seemed merely curious about the intruders. On the main staircase voices called out, "Who are you?" and "Why are you here?" In the library the leader's hand was innocently grabbed by a small child. But the longer they remained, the more active — and upset — the spirits became.

In the basement they witnessed objects being moved

on their own and heard a voice warn them to *leave now*. Unheeding the advice, the ghost hunters travelled up to the old dorm rooms where, if the story is to be believed, the girls who murdered Angela would have spent their nights. The visitors described the area as a hot spot for dark entities, all identifiable as teenage girls. The group used a digital recorder that, when played back, revealed so many voices overlapping each other that much of what was said couldn't be understood. But the words that cut through the ruckus were foul, abusive and threatening. Sticks and stones may break your bones, but so would a hard shove at the top of the stairs. And the dead girls repeatedly tried to trip and push the living intruders in this part of the building.

Stairs leading to the main floor and basement

Today the grounds where Alma College once stood with pride are empty except for shattered bricks and burnt wood. Although you'll never be able to climb the Ivory Tower and ask Angela if she's still there, or brave the dangerously haunted dormitory, it's said that the ghosts of Alma College still linger amidst the rubble of the grandiose building. In this light, the college's motto is fitting:

Though we are far from thee
Still we long for thee
Ever loyal still

FED INTO THE FURNACE

Edmonton, Alberta

You might think that a gruesome murder story and a resident ghost might be bad for a hotel's business, but for La Bohème in Edmonton, the opposite is true. Every Halloween the building is booked to capacity with guests hoping to catch a glimpse of the spectre that has terrorized many people over the years.

Built in 1912, La Bohème was originally a luxury three-storey apartment building with shops on the main floor before being converted into a bed and breakfast in 1982. The story of the murder that happened while it was an apartment building is so horrific, so grisly, that the faint of heart might not want to read any further.

Still with me?

Don't say I didn't warn you.

As co-owner and caretaker Mike Comeau and his ghost-hunting guests will tell you, the legend goes like this: the original caretaker murdered his wife on the top floor of the building and dragged her body by the feet down three flights of stairs. Then, in the dark, dingy basement, he fed her corpse into the furnace. But in order to make it fit, he had to chop it up into tiny pieces.

Since that day people have had terrifying experiences in the building. Guests have been woken in the middle of the night by the *thud, thud, thud* sound of a head banging down the stairs, only to rush into the hallway, turn on a light and see . . . an empty staircase.

Larry Finnson, a businessman and regular guest at La Bohème, had a particularly scary experience one night. While staying in Suite 7, the most haunted room, he woke up to find his bed levitating in mid-air.

Furnace of La Bohème

The murdered woman's ghost has also bothered employees of the bed and breakfast. One woman was alone doing laundry in the basement next to the furnace room when she was suddenly grabbed from behind. Comeau says she was so petrified that she ran screaming up the stairs and straight out the front door, never to return.

Have a flip through La Bohème's guest book and you'll find otherworldly accounts forever etched in history by the hotel's visitors, such as the couple who saw a beautiful woman in their closet at night, a woman whose feet had been severed from her legs.

Given the claims of what a previous caretaker used it for, you might be surprised to learn that the original furnace is still being used to heat the building today. If you visit La Bohème it'll keep you warm through the night, even when your blood turns to ice.

DINING WITH THE DEAD

Halifax, Nova Scotia

Standing proudly on the busy downtown corner of Carmichael and Argyle Streets, the Five Fishermen Restaurant is one of Halifax's busiest dining locations. But it's not only bustling during open hours — some customers don't wish to leave after it closes for the night. These customers don't require much service from the wait staff. You see, they don't eat anything and have a habit of disappearing into thin air when approached.

The brick-and-wood building was built in 1817 as a schoolhouse before becoming the Halifax Victorian School of Art. The school was run by Anna Leonowens in the years after she served as governess to the children of the King of Siam, which was made famous in the musical film *The King and I*. Despite this claim to fame, the school closed in the late 1800s and the building became even more famous — or rather, *infamous*.

In 1883 the building was converted into the John Snow & Co. Funeral Home, setting the stage for its morbid destiny.

On April 14, 1912, the RMS *Titanic* struck an iceberg during its maiden voyage from the United Kingdom to New York City. It sank a little less than three hours later in the North Atlantic Ocean, six hundred kilometres south of Newfoundland. It was the largest ship afloat at the time and its passengers were some of the wealthiest in the world. The sinking of the RMS *Titanic* was one of the deadliest maritime disasters in modern history, claiming the lives of more than fifteen hundred passengers. As the nearest mainland port, Halifax served as the home base for the rescue operations, and most of the bodies were brought to John Snow & Co. Funeral Home.

Five short years later, still reeling from the shock of the *Titanic's* sinking, Nova Scotia was dealt another tragedy of unfathomable magnitude: the Halifax explosion. On December 6, 1917, a French cargo ship loaded with wartime explosives struck a second ship near Halifax Harbour. Twenty minutes later a fire ignited the cargo, creating the largest man-made explosion prior to the creation of nuclear weapons. The blast decimated an entire district of downtown Halifax, and flying debris, collapsing buildings and fires killed approximately two thousand people and injured nine thousand others. Once again, many of the dead were taken to the John Snow & Co. Funeral Home.

Having served as the final destination for so many victims of two of the modern world's greatest disasters, it's no wonder many people are struck by an unexplainable energy as soon as they set foot inside. But after the building changed hands once again and opened as the Five Fishermen Restaurant in 1975, customers unaware of the history might not be expecting a side of fright with their foie gras.

The spooky stories restaurant employees have shared are so numerous that they could nearly fill an entire book on their own. The staff are so accustomed to the spirits they work with that they no longer bat an eye when glasses fly from shelves, water taps turn on and off or cutlery lifts off tables and crashes on the floor. It's common for the staff to hear their names whispered in their ears when they're all alone. One employee once rushed into a private room called the Captain's Quarters because he heard a man and a woman arguing, only to find the room empty. Servers have seen a misty grey apparition float down the stairs to the kitchen as they were closing the restaurant. Even more disconcerting was the time a server heard a tapping sound upon a second floor window, which was especially odd since nothing on ground level could reach the window. When she approached to investigate, she saw the same misty grey apparition hovering outside in the air.

Then there's the man, old and tall with long grey hair, dressed in a black greatcoat from another time. He's been spotted a few times, most notably by a young man whose task it was to prepare the salad bar before the dinner rush. One warm summer day he was carrying crates of vegetables to the bar when he heard a loud crash nearby. Unsure what could have caused the commotion — he was alone in the restaurant at the time — he set the vegetables down and wandered around the dining area. On the floor he found a shattered ashtray, which he knelt down to examine. When he stood back up he happened to look in a mirror, and in it he saw the old man in the long black coat walking toward him from behind. The young man dropped the ashtray and spun around, but the grey-haired man had disappeared.

You might have noticed that a common thread running through these stories is that the paranormal activity only occurs when there aren't any customers in the restaurant, but that's not always the case.

One evening a group of diners tried to send a text message from their table, but only one word — which the diners hadn't typed — was sent to the recipient of the message: DEATH.

Another particularly busy night, the hostess was walking a couple to their table. As they crossed the dining room she suddenly felt something hit her across the

John Snow & Co., second building from right, with coffins for victims of the Halifax explosion stacked outside

face, but she couldn't detect the cause, so she assumed it was her imagination. After seating the couple, the hostess returned to the restaurant's entrance where the maître d' looked at her gravely and asked in a hushed tone, "What happened to your face?"

There, across the hostess's cheek, as if she'd been slapped, was an angry red handprint.

WHERE HORROR AND HOCKEY SHARE A HOME

Toronto, Ontario

One bright and cheery summer day, a young boy toured the Hockey Hall of Fame with a group of adults. Like the three hundred thousand people who visit every year, the boy enjoyed the displays featuring Maurice "The Rocket" Richard and Wayne Gretzky, tested his own skills in the NHLPA Be a Player Zone and marvelled at the Stanley Cup up close.

Suddenly, as he passed through one of the exhibits, the boy stopped dead in his tracks. His rigid stance and wide eyes were so odd and out of place that the adults wondered what could possibly be wrong with him. Then, with a trembling hand, he pointed at an empty wall.

"What is it?" they asked him.

"Don't you see her?" he screamed over and over and

over. "Don't you see her? Don't you see her? Don't you see her?"

There was no one there. "See who?" they asked fearfully.

Jane Rodney, who was the Hall's coordinator of resource centre services at the time, says the boy saw a woman with long black hair pass back and forth through the wall as if daring him to look away.

The description matched that of Dorothea "Dorothy" Mae Elliott, the Hockey Hall of Fame's resident ghost. The boy is only one of two people who have seen Dorothy's ghost, but plenty of others have had terrifying experiences and witnessed paranormal activity in the building since 1953. That was the year Dorothy died in the women's washroom from a self-inflicted gunshot wound.

Before the Hockey Hall of Fame opened in 1993, the grand building that stands out among the contemporary skyscrapers was a branch of the Bank of Montreal for nearly one hundred years. Dorothy was a bank teller and, by her co-workers' accounts, she was beautiful, sociable and very popular. But it was whispered around the bank that she was harbouring a dark secret. It was believed she was having an affair with a married man, either another teller or one of the branch managers. Perhaps this transgression is what led her to take her own life.

Co-worker Doreen Bracken arrived on the fateful day at 8:00 a.m. and was surprised to find Dorothy already at work looking tired, unkempt and depressed. At 9:00 a.m. another employee began screaming over the balcony of the second floor. Doreen and others raced upstairs and found Dorothy on the floor of the women's washroom, a puddle of blood quickly spreading across the floor. Beside her body was the bank's revolver, a .38 calibre that tellers were expected to use in case of a robbery.

Shortly thereafter signs of Dorothy's lingering spirit were witnessed by the staff. The women refused to use the second floor washroom. They felt a presence within, an unpleasant one, like they were being watched. Management finally gave in and had a new washroom built in the basement, but unexplainable occurrences persisted. Lights flickered on and off. Objects disappeared and reappeared mysteriously. Locked doors and windows suddenly flew open of their own accord.

Custodial workers have had some of the most frightening experiences while working alone through the night. When all is dark and quiet, footsteps creak along the floorboards overhead, moans and shrieks echo from the second floor and some have even felt phantom hands grab and push them from behind.

Rob Hynes, who was previously the Hockey Hall of Fame special events supervisor, witnessed something he'll never forget. He was in the building early one morning preparing for an event. Suddenly he had the unusual feeling that someone was watching him. The odd sensation drew him into a pitch-black room on the second floor where the sensation was the strongest. What happened inside the room was unexpected and terrifying. A chair was spinning in circles as if caught in the middle of a small cyclone. Suddenly the chair slid across the floor and right into his hand. Despite the fact that Hynes is skeptical when it comes to ghosts, he wasted no time fleeing the room.

Other than the young boy, the other person who saw Dorothy's ghost in the metaphorical flesh is Joanna Jordan, a Toronto musician. She was commissioned to play the harp in the Great Hall during an event. She was unaware that the building had a haunted history, so she wasn't prepared at all when she looked up and saw Dorothy's ghost floating just below the second floor ceiling, looking down upon her intently. To this day the image of the black-haired woman staring at her from the ceiling is as vivid in Joanna's memory as on the day she saw Dorothy. She returned to the building a few years later but, try as she might, she couldn't head up to the second floor.

Our country's national sport can be a hard-hitting, aggressive game filled with fights, body checks, bruisers and goons. It's fitting that the Hockey Hall of Fame is home to a presence more chilling than a few hours spent outdoors playing pond hockey in the middle of January.

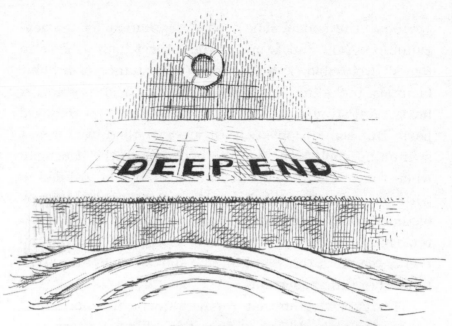

THE BOY IN THE BASEMENT

New Westminster, British Columbia

A school is supposed to be a place for learning, a place where children feel safe, a place to grow. It's not supposed to be a place where a boy in the basement relives his death over and over.

But then New Westminster Secondary School has a morbid history dating back to its construction. The site where the school now sits was used in the mid to late 1800s as a cemetery for marginalized groups of the day, including Chinese pioneers, Indigenous people, convicted criminals and the mentally handicapped. The school was built in 1949, and the cemetery was found when a bull-dozer unearthed an unmarked coffin. But nothing was done about the ghastly discovery, and construction of the school continued.

Today the school has a good reputation for its academic program and is one of the largest high schools in British Columbia. It also has an abundance of athletic facilities, including four gyms, a football field, two soccer fields, a skating rink, a fitness room and a skateboard park. But some people contest whether there was ever a swimming pool. Some say the pool was in the basement when the school first opened but it's since been filled in with concrete. Others believe the pool only exists as part of the school's lore. Regardless of what New Westminster residents believe, one thing most of the school's alumni can agree on is that the building has a creepy vibe, particularly in the basement.

The reports claim that a male student drowned in the pool in the early 1970s and that it was filled in years later due to safety concerns. In the time between the drowning and the pool's closure, however, security guards regularly saw a boy floating face down in the water during their nightly rounds. They would turn to grab a pole or call for help, but when they turned back the boy would be gone and the water perfectly still. These reports from the guards seem to support the existence of the pool at one time in the school's history.

Guards have also reported similar paranormal activity in the archery range, also located in the basement. A man is said to have been seen firing a phantom bow and arrows, only to disappear when anyone got too close.

Another male student is said to have died in the 1980s in the school's woodworking shop, which, unlike the pool, is definitely still in operation today. No one has reported coming face to face with the woodworking boy, but he has been spotted by night guards on the security camera monitors. When they run to the room, the boy is gone.

Even the music room isn't immune to paranormal activity, as the school's cameras have also picked up unexplained glowing orbs hovering in the air.

Just like the existence of the pool in the basement, some people believe that the reports of the deaths in the school have been fabricated. If they're right, it's possible that all the ghostly sightings in New Westminster Secondary School over the years can be attributed to the bones that unceremoniously clog the dirt beneath the building's foundation.

THE LADY IN BLUE

Peggy's Cove, Nova Scotia

The ocean is known for its mesmerizing beauty that's as dangerous as it is breathtaking. It's widely believed among ghost enthusiasts that a soul who perishes in the water is likely to meet such a traumatic end that he or she has a difficult time moving on and finding peace. When that soul willingly drowns in the deep blue, committing suicide, the likelihood of a haunting is even greater. A legend from one of Atlantic Canada's most popular tourist destinations confirms this belief.

Located forty-four kilometres southwest of Halifax, Peggy's Cove is a small fishing village known for its photographic beauty, quaint homes and the Peggy's Point Lighthouse, one of Canada's most iconic images. Strict land-use laws have maintained the idyllic atmosphere of

Peggy's Cove, preventing rapid property development and keeping the population to a mere six hundred people. Although the inhabitants still fish for lobster, tourism has become more economically important to the community than fishing. The tourists come to see the boats, the lobster traps and the famous lighthouse, but many are confronted by something they hadn't planned on seeing: The Lady in Blue, an ethereal spirit that walks the shoreline. She's such a sad vision that it might chill your heart and make your blood run cold simply to look at her.

A few legends have popped up to explain her existence. The most popular is that a woman named Margaret lived in the area in the 1700s before it was called Peggy's Cove. The source of the name of the village isn't documented, so some believe it comes from nearby Saint Margaret's Bay ("Peggy" is a nickname of Margaret), which Samuel de Champlain named after his mother, Marguerite. But others believe that it's named after Margaret, The Lady in Blue. It's said she was the sole survivor of a shipwreck in 1800, a disaster that claimed the lives of everyone onboard, including her young children, but spared her. She'd walk the shores for days on end, her blue dress rippling in the wind and her eyes scanning the Atlantic Ocean. Little did Margaret know that, while she watched the water, Death was watching her.

Her second husband, in an attempt to cure his wife's depression, joined her one day on the rocky shore. He stepped in front of her and danced a jig, hoping to amuse Margaret, maybe even make her smile or laugh. But his foot slipped, he fell, his head cracked against the rocks and he died a quick, bloody death.

The grief from back-to-back tragedies was too much for poor Margaret to bear. She was seen one day shortly after

The lighthouse at Peggy's Cove

the death of her husband walking into the ocean . . . and was never seen again.

Well, not *alive*.

The ghost of Margaret — or Peggy of the Cove, as she's become known — has become a permanent resident of the small fishing village. Since the lighthouse was built in 1868, The Lady in Blue has been spotted forever wandering the rocky shores at its base. Some say she looks like she's about to jump into the Atlantic, others claim she's spoken softly to them, but everyone agrees: she's not a threatening or frightening ghost, but a deeply sad one. Like the relentless crash of cool blue waves upon the shore, Margaret's soul will never give up the search for the family she lost.

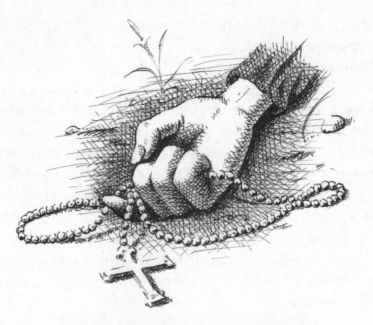

THE HAUNTED HOTEL

Victoria, British Columbia

Spend a night in The Fairmont Empress Hotel and chances are you won't be spending the night alone. Unexpected guests — the type of guests who can pass *through* doors instead of needing to open them — have a habit of haunting the halls and bedrooms in this grand hotel.

With nearly five hundred rooms and an imposing presence overlooking Victoria's Inner Harbour, The Empress is one of the oldest and most famous hotels in British Columbia. Since it opened in 1908 it has welcomed kings, queens, movie stars and other notable celebrities, including *The Jungle Book* author Rudyard Kipling. It's little wonder some souls never want to leave, even after all earthly ties have been severed from their bodies.

A carpenter is likely the ghost that's been haunting

The Empress for the longest time. It's said the worker hanged himself from the rafters of the west wing during the hotel's construction, two years before it opened. For as long as The Empress has been open to the public, countless guests have reported seeing a man with bulging eyes and a thick rope cutting into his neck swaying from the roof. It's not known why the carpenter committed suicide, but if you pass through the West Wing late at night, don't look up — you might not like what you see.

The carpenter has been hanging out in the hotel for a little longer than the spirit of Lizzie McGrath, a chambermaid who worked and lived in the hotel when it opened. She lived in a room on the sixth floor, which used to be designated for chambermaids. Lizzie was a devout Irish Catholic and by all accounts a hard worker. She had a habit of stepping out of her room and onto the fire escape after a long, arduous day cleaning The Empress's many guest rooms. Under the pale glow of the moon, she'd clear her head and complete her rosary. The night air revitalized her body and her faith, giving her peace. In 1909, when the first addition was being added to the hotel, the fire escapes were removed so they wouldn't be in the way of construction. But no one told poor Lizzie. Unbeknownst to her, she completed what would be her final (living) day of work, returned to her room, grabbed her rosary beads and stepped outside, falling six storeys to her death. Construction workers rolled her body over early the next morning. Clutched tightly in her hands were her beloved rosary beads.

Lizzie's hard-working attitude has extended into the afterlife, and her ghost is often seen on the sixth floor, still carrying out her cleaning duties.

At least Lizzie's spirit seems to be at home, so to speak.

The Fairmont Empress Hotel

The ghost of another woman stuck in The Empress isn't so lucky. Many guests have been awoken by loud, frantic pounding on their doors in the middle of the night. In the hall, panicked and disoriented, is a lost woman in pajamas who pleads for help. Leading guests by her icy-cold hand, she takes them to the elevator . . . and then simply disappears. It's believed she used to haunt a room that was demolished to build a new elevator and is now left to wander the hotel's halls, forever looking for her room, forever lost.

But the hotel's most famous ghost is its architect, Francis Rattenbury, whose final days were mired in controversy. Following the opening of The Empress, Rattenbury became a well-known and respected public figure in Victoria, but he tarnished his reputation when he left his wife and children to marry a woman, Alma, who was less than half his age. Following a string of bad investments and the stress of the scandal, Rattenbury was murdered in his drawing-room in England, his skull cracked open by either a carpenter's hammer or croquet mallet (the reports of the weapon vary). His chauffeur, George, was charged and convicted of the murder, and it was revealed that George and Alma had been a secret couple for some time. Shortly after Rattenbury was murdered, Alma took her own life, stabbing a knife into her broken heart.

Rattenbury, it would appear, wishes to remain in the hotel he designed, reliving his glory days before he made a string of poor choices that ultimately led to his untimely death. He wanders The Empress's halls, keeping an eye on his crowning achievement and its many guests — many of whom are, like Rattenbury, long since deceased.

THE HANGMAN'S KNOT

Quebec City, Quebec

Place Royale is not only a beautifully quaint and historic square in the heart of Old Quebec, it's also considered to be the birthplace of New France. Founded in 1608 by French navigator and explorer Samuel de Champlain, the area first served as a bustling fur marketplace and is home to Notre-Dame-des-Victoires, the oldest stone church in North America. But behind the charming facade of the heritage buildings and cobblestone streets lies a violent past that has ensnared its fair share of spirits.

Today, Place Royale is a must-see destination for tourists, many of whom step off one of the many cruise ships that dock in nearby Old Port for a little sightseeing. But even travellers desperate to stretch their legs after a long sea voyage might not spend too long on land before hurrying back to their ships after nightfall. The man in the shadows who watches all who pass through Place Royale's gates and the woman who hauntingly roams around the Notre-Dame-des-Victoires church each and every night are neither tourists nor locals. Well, they're not locals to *present*-day Place Royale, seeing as they were both killed in the 1600s.

In addition to the hustle and bustle of the trading that took place in the market square, Place Royale was also where men, women and children found guilty of crimes were executed in brutal fashion. And even those found guilty of minor crimes were given a one-way ticket to visit the hangman, including the very first person executed in Quebec City: a 16-year-old girl charged with petty theft.

One short month after Champlain established Place Royale, he caught wind of a plot to murder him. He received a covert report that four men, led by locksmith Jean Duval, planned to deliver the slain Champlain and Quebec into the hands of the Spanish for their own profit. Armed with this information, Champlain struck first and invited the four men to his house for dinner. Thinking it would be the perfect opportunity to complete their murderous plan, Duval and the others accepted the invitation and arrived at his doorstep. But before they could harm Champlain, he had them arrested for treason. The three followers were sent to France to be executed, but Champlain had a special plan for their ringleader. Duval was hanged beside Place Royale's gate, but that wasn't enough to deter copycats. Duval's lifeless body was then beheaded before the crowd. His head was deposited on a pike and placed atop the highest rooftop. His blank stare upon the square below served as a constant warning against treason. His ghost — a shadowy figure spotted by

Notre-Dame-des-Victoires

many tourists after nightfall — has taken up permanent residence near the gate where his body once swayed at the end of a rope.

If it's any consolation for the ghost of Duval, he's had another executed criminal's spirit to keep him company in Place Royale. In 1680, not long after Duval was hanged and decapitated, a new executioner was appointed. Jean Gatier was advised to move with his wife and small children out of the city so that he wouldn't live amongst the very people he might one day need to kill. He did so willingly, never imagining that, regardless of how far he lived from the city limits, he would still be living with someone he would one day execute.

Shortly after they moved far from Place Royale, his wife was convicted of stealing goods from a merchant. Her sentence was death by hanging. The executioner was forced to do the heartbreaking task, hanging his own wife and the mother of his children in front of Notre-Dame-des-Victoires church. The apparition of Madame Gatier still wanders the cobblestone alleyways in Place Royale, eternally searching for her husband. Whether she pines for a reunion or revenge is unknown.

THE WATER GHOST

Holland Cove, Prince Edward Island

Prince Edward Island is well known as the setting of Lucy Maud Montgomery's beloved *Anne of Green Gables*. The beauty of P.E.I.'s rolling green hills and red, sandy beaches set the perfect stage for Montgomery's stories, which are worldwide bestsellers. It's fitting that a province known around the globe for its idyllic "island life" would be the home of a waterlogged ghost that rises with the tide.

Each year on July 14, when the tide is at its highest point, inhabitants of Holland Cove report seeing a woman appear from the murky depths of the water. She's dressed in a white gown and her long black hair hangs heavily from her scalp. Once on land she leaves a wet trail in her wake that never stops flowing from her body. She wanders up and down the beach, her wet eyes filled with sadness, and calls, "Samuel? Samuel?" Never finding the man she seeks, she eventually wanders back into the water to drown herself. Year after year she resurfaces, searches in vain for Samuel, then commits her body to the waves once more. Year after year no body is ever recovered from the surf.

Who is she, and who is Samuel? These are questions that all who have come face to face with the water ghost have asked themselves for a long, long time. Most believe the man she's in search of is none other than Captain Samuel Johannes Holland, the namesake of Holland Cove. Appointed Surveyor General of North America by the British, Captain Holland came to the area in 1764 and spent the next two years creating detailed maps that are still in use today. Captain Holland fell in love with Canada and spent the rest of his days here before his death in 1801.

Holland Cove

The legend states that the ghost is Captain Holland's wife, a beautiful woman named Racine who came from French royalty. One wintry day on the cove, Captain Holland was late returning home from an expedition. Fearing the worst, Racine carelessly ventured out onto the ice in hopes of seeing her husband, but the ice was too thin and it cracked. Racine plummeted into the icy water and drowned. Captain Holland returned shortly thereafter to the heartbreaking news, but it wasn't long before he was reunited with his deceased bride. He reported seeing her a few days later, soaked to the bone and deathly pale, wailing and calling his name, before vanishing in front of his very eyes.

The story doesn't hold much water due to some large holes. First, the ghost appears every summer, but Racine supposedly died in the winter — it's common lore for ghosts to appear on the date of their death. Some believe this can be explained by the high tide, which might spew her spirit to the beach much like a piece of driftwood.

The larger problem is that Captain Holland was married twice but neither wife was named Racine. His second wife, the one who lived with him at Holland Cove, Marie-Joseph Rollet, was French as the legend suggests. It's possible "Racine" was a nickname. However, Marie-Joseph outlived her husband, so it's unlikely the ghost can be attributed to her if the story is to be believed.

The true identity of the water ghost might never be determined, but that won't stop the tide from rising. Every July the water ghost is sure to emerge from the ocean, water draining from her every pore as she laments the loss of Samuel. And whether or not you believe in the legend of Racine and Captain Holland, you'd be well advised to heed one piece of advice those familiar with the tale hasten to add: if you hear the water ghost of Holland Cove, don't venture anywhere near her. It's believed everyone who lays eyes on her will one day drown as well.

DEAD AND BURIED, BUT NOT GONE

St. John's, Newfoundland and Labrador

Some buildings inspire fear the moment you spot them. Others are trickier and don't immediately stand out, like they're trying to hide a secret or erase the past. One such location is the Cathedral Street Bistro in downtown St. John's. On the surface it's a charming restaurant offering fine dining, a small red building attached to a larger blue one that was at one time rented out for use as apartments. But appearances can be deceiving, and the stories about the Cathedral Street Bistro point to the building's eerie, hidden history.

A number of businesses were located in the building before the Cathedral Street Bistro opened, including other restaurants, an inn and the aforementioned apartments. But it also used to be a funeral home dating back to 1891, the final earthly stop for many a soul, and many believe the ghosts that still dwell within the restaurant date back to that time. Some even believe the negative energy of the living people who visited the funeral home to grieve the loss of a loved one is soaked into the walls like a stain that can't be washed clean. Whatever one decides to believe, there's no question that the stories told in hushed tones about the Cathedral Street Bistro are frightening.

Brian Abbott owned and operated Chez Briann, one of the restaurants that occupied the building before the Cathedral Street Bistro opened. He knows of at least two spirits that have haunted its halls. One day an employee began to walk down the stairs when she saw something and stopped. There was a person at the bottom of the staircase, but the figure appeared to be made more of smoke than flesh and bone. Suddenly the misty spectre flew up the stairs and passed straight through her.

The other ghost his staff encountered regularly was an old man who dwelled in the dining room when the restaurant was quiet. He had a stern face and ice-cold eyes, and would catch your stare as if challenging you to look away or run. That's exactly what the wait staff would do. For every time they held his stare for more than a few seconds he would begin to approach them. No one ever stuck around long enough to discover the stern man's intentions.

It's certainly not the type of place you'd want to spend the night, but of course, that's exactly what people did when the building was the Victoria Station Inn during the 1990s. One night a woman woke up with severe pain in her chest. Floating above her was a ghost, an old man, quite possibly the same one that would later be seen by restaurant staff. She lay paralyzed in her bed, unable to blink and forced to watch as the man placed two coins over her eyes. The act of placing two coins on a dead body's eyelids is an old custom based on the belief that the departed would need the money to pay a boatman to carry the body across the river Styx. But this woman was still alive. Either the man was mistaken or his actions hinted at darker plans. Fortunately, the woman regained control of her body and was able to escape before the ghost could harm her.

Others have reported seeing a lost spirit, this time a woman, wandering the halls in the middle of the night. She doesn't speak or approach anyone, but those who have gotten close enough have seen a distinguishing characteristic that never fails to chill the blood: running down the length of her torso is a jagged scar, as if from a recent autopsy.

It's unsettling to think that, as guests wine and dine in the restaurant, it's still business as usual for the funeral home that closed its doors long ago. But the spirits of those who worked there or were prepared for burial within have no intention of going quietly into the night.

THE BLUE GHOST TUNNEL

Thorold, Ontario

There lies an old stone tunnel in the woods of Thorold. It's crumbling, dark and dangerous; abandoned, remote and difficult to find. Many people — even with detailed directions — become turned around and never find it. That's probably for the best. Something dwells in the darkness, something that becomes violent and angry when disturbed.

The tales told by those who have reached the tunnel should be enough to deter others from seeking it out. A young man named Justin explored it with a friend before Halloween one year. They were both armed with a brand-new flashlight and freshly charged batteries but still felt a deep sense of dread as soon as they approached the tunnel's wide, gaping mouth. Inside, the tunnel was so dark they couldn't see their hands before their faces, so they decided to turn on their flashlights. Only one would work. Justin was left quite literally in the dark, all too reliant upon his friend's light to see.

They heard voices coming from the deep, so the friend went farther in to investigate. Justin waited anxiously behind. He tried not to think of the suffocating blackness that surrounded him like a cloud of smoke. The only sound he could hear was a *drip-drip-drip* of water falling from the tunnel's roof. He faced the direction his friend had left and saw an approaching light. But just then his friend appeared — not in front of him, but at his side. The friend had walked the length of the tunnel and no one was there. So who, or what, was holding the light they could see? Before much longer the light disappeared. That was enough to force them out of the tunnel.

Standing outside the entrance, regretting their decision to venture into the tunnel at all, they suddenly heard a piercing scream echo from within. Justin took the flashlight from his friend, pointed it at the darkness and turned it on . . . but the light that had worked moments ago faded out.

Their courage faded away too. They left immediately without exploring any further, putting as much distance between them and the tunnel as possible.

Sometime later, a woman named Lori entered the tunnel with a group of friends, hoping for a bit of a thrill. She found more than she had hoped for. Deep in the tunnel the group stopped and silently waited for something to happen. Without warning, a small hand grabbed Lori's and pulled her from behind.

"Which one of you did that?" she asked her friends, but no one was close enough to have touched her. Just then her other hand was yanked by something in the shadows.

"Help," a small child's voice whispered in her ear.

Lori wasn't the only one to hear the ghostly plea; her friends heard it too. They all began to feel oddly exhausted and wearily left the tunnel. The next day many of the group were physically ill, as if they'd somehow been infected by the tunnel's air.

A man named Mark has trekked into the tunnel many times over the years and had a few creepy encounters, including hearing whispers from the walls and a woman crying. These haunting sounds weren't enough to keep him away permanently, but one night when exploring with a friend, he had such a terrifying encounter that he hasn't been back since. Mark and his friend split up to explore opposite ends of the tunnel. Walking slowly in silence, Mark came to a low wooden beam. He ducked to pass below it, and when he stood up on the other side he was immediately confronted by an angry spirit that moved toward him. The ghost was an old man in outdated clothing. His face was twisted with rage and he pointed his cane threateningly at Mark. The moment the spirit was close enough to strike he vanished. Then came a loud thump and the sound of footsteps running in the opposite direction. Mark's friend returned and confirmed he had heard the bang and the footsteps. Mark was shaking badly and was absolutely petrified. He had felt the man's anger and hate radiating off his dead body in waves. He somehow knew the ghost was mad at the intrusion and was trying to protect the tunnel.

Originally called the Merritton Tunnel, it was built in the mid-1870s to provide passage beneath a canal for trains of the Great Western Railway. But the construction was plagued by many serious injuries and three reported deaths. One such tragedy occurred when some of the heavy limestone rocks used to create the tunnel's walls fell on top of a fourteen-year-old Irish immigrant, crushing him to death.

The Welland Canal construction project, which was being completed at the same time, also resulted in several fatalities, many of which occurred directly above the Merritton Tunnel site. The further expansion of the canal system in the 1920s required that an old abandoned church be demolished and the skeletal inhabitants of the cemetery be moved to create a reservoir. There were 913 graves in the cemetery, but it's estimated only 250 were actually located and moved, leaving 663 corpses at the bottom of the water located very close to the tunnel's entrance.

As if that weren't enough, there was also a horrible, head-on collision between two trains near the western entrance of the tunnel on January 3, 1902. The collision claimed the lives of each of the trains' firemen. Abraham Desult received burns to ninety percent of his body and was rushed to St. Catharines General Hospital, where he died five hours after the accident. Charles Horning was killed instantly. His body was crushed and mangled between the boiler and a large piece of ironwork.

A mere eleven years after it had been completed, the tunnel was deemed too dangerous for frequent passage and converted to occasional use. Then, in 1915, it was closed completely. Without the passage of trains it became a ghost tunnel, both figuratively and literally. But where did it get its present-day nickname, the Blue Ghost Tunnel?

In 1999 a teenager named Russ heard rumours about the tunnel's haunted history from a friend. Russ had started a website that listed haunted locations in the Niagara

Inside the Merritton Tunnel

Falls region and decided to visit the Merritton Tunnel to see for himself if anything sinister dwelled within. With the company of three friends — safety, they hoped, in numbers — Russ approached the tunnel's entrance. The members of the group suddenly felt dizzy, as if electrical currents were surging through their bodies. It seemed like something was trying to keep them away. Before they decided whether to enter the tunnel or leave, an icy blue, fog-like apparition materialized in front of them. The entity shifted in form — first a screaming face, then a human body, next a wolf and finally a demon. It blocked their path for fifteen long seconds before disappearing. Despite the fact that they had visited the tunnel to see a ghost, they admitted to being overcome by fear. No one could find the courage to enter. They agreed that the blue ghost they had all seen was guarding the entrance and would not allow them to enter without terrible consequences. When Russ reported this petrifying confrontation online, the Blue Ghost Tunnel's notoriety grew exponentially.

Despite the tunnel's sinister reputation — or maybe because of it — people keep visiting it in the middle of the night. Most of the time, they see or hear something horrifying. And more often than not, they run away as quickly as possible, never to return.

ISLE OF DEMONS

Quirpon Island, Newfoundland and Labrador

The year was 1544 and Marguerite de La Rocque gripped an old, chipped sword in her hand. The dull blade was her last line of defence against the pack of wolves that closed in on all sides. She sliced the air between them with the sword and screamed at the wild animals. The wolves answered with howls and snarls, their lips pulled back and their hackles raised. Wind whipped Marguerite's long, tangled hair across her weathered and gaunt face. At her heels were the recently covered graves of her boyfriend, her lady servant and, most heartbreakingly, her newborn son. The wolves were mad with hunger. There was little to eat on the island and they wanted what was in those graves. In the bone-chillingly cold night on the uninhabited Isle of Demons, dressed in the skins of bears she herself had killed and skinned, Marguerite was virtually indistinguishable from the beasts that closed in on her. She had become a wild animal herself.

Had anyone seen her at that moment, it would have been impossible to believe that, only two years before, she had been part of France's high society, a woman of distinguished birth and wealth. How Marguerite came to be marooned on an island teeming with dangerous animals, demons and evil spirits, fighting for her life, is a tragic story. It's so far-fetched it seems like fantasy, but truth is often stranger than fiction.

In the summer of 1542, Marguerite was accompanying her uncle, Jean-François de La Rocque de Roberval, on a ship full of passengers from France to colonize the Canadian wilderness. Among the other passengers willing to make the voyage and start a new life was Etienne Gosselin, the son of a notary, who had a passion for the sea that made him want nothing more than to be a shipbuilder. Fair-haired and pale, young Marguerite had led a sheltered life as a French maiden and was instantly attracted to Etienne when they met aboard the ship. Etienne, with curly hair and eyes as blue as the sea, entertained the ship's passengers by playing his zither, a stringed instrument. When he sang a long and romantic song that he had written about Marguerite, their relationship and fate were both sealed. But neither would have a happy ending.

They began courting in secret. Her servant, Damienne, was the only other person who was aware of their relationship. Secrets, however, are as hard to hide on a ship as an elephant in a small room. Jean-François soon found out. He felt betrayed and hurt, and as a God-fearing man he believed that the secret union would anger the Lord. He kept both his rage and fear hidden, biding his time before acting against his niece in a cold and calculated fashion. As Marguerite's legal guardian, financially strapped Jean-François had nothing to gain should she marry Etienne, and everything to lose. On the other hand, if Marguerite were to die — not by Jean-François' hands, of course — before a wedding could take place, Jean-François would inherit a large sum of money.

Long days passed. The ship arrived in Canada and sailed along the coast of Newfoundland. Jean-François leaned against the railing and stared at the lands they passed. And then he spotted what he had been looking for: the Isle of Demons.

This legendary land, believed to be located in present-day Quirpon Island, first appeared on maps in 1508 and was found on nautical charts until the mid-seventeenth century. It was populated by so many demons and ghosts that passing ships gave the island a wide berth and the few hardened men who went ashore did so with crucifixes clutched tightly in their shaking hands. The apparitions that haunted the island were the tortured souls who had drowned in the Atlantic Ocean. They were reported to make terrible noises while leading the living astray. Fierce carnivores like bears and wolves roamed the land, and the winters were colder than cold. It was not a place any human could live.

Jean-François's plan was to maroon his niece on the Isle of Demons as punishment for her sins, under the guise of allowing God to determine her fate, but it was nothing short of a death sentence.

Without hesitation he informed his crew of this decision and ordered his niece to leave the ship immediately, along with Damienne for her part in the conspiracy. He left them some rifles and supplies and then, ignoring her pleas, set sail without pause so that no one would have time to take pity on Marguerite and try to rescue her.

When Etienne discovered what was happening, he rushed to the deck with his own loaded rifle and insisted that he be allowed to join Marguerite and Damienne. Jean-François had intended to maroon him later on a different island but decided to grant him his foolish wish. He had some men from his crew ferry Etienne to the island in a small boat with further supplies and taunted the young couple as the ship sailed away.

Once the ship and her uncle had disappeared over the horizon, Marguerite, Etienne and Damienne quickly got to work. For shelter they built a crude wooden hut near a cavern. They hunted small animals and searched for berries and herbs they could eat. There were no other people on the island, just rocks, sand and deep forests, but for a while it seemed like they'd be okay. Hopefully they'd be able to survive long enough for another ship to pass by. Then night fell. And with the night came the creatures.

The wind carried supernatural voices, so loud and threatening that it seemed to the terrified trio that there were more than one hundred thousand angry men approaching. Ghosts flitted in and out of the fog that ensnared their hut like a heavy blanket. Red eyes peered in at them through gaps in the wood and hands and claws, both human and animal, tried to pry the boards apart. The voices laughed and howled and cackled, and the shapes of the demons and apparitions besieging them shifted and morphed before their eyes.

Nearly faint with fear, Marguerite, Etienne and Damienne repented their sins and read aloud from the Bible. Miraculously, this was enough to diminish the attacks, although the creatures didn't leave them alone for long. As the days passed they had to remain vigilant to protect themselves against the evil shades that were hidden in every dark corner of the island and grew active after nightfall.

Days turned into weeks and weeks turned into months, yet no rescue party came to their salvation. Ships did pass but quickly fled from the sight of people waving their arms and sending smoke into the sky, people who looked less human by the day. With a sickening feeling, Marguerite realized that from the water they must look exactly like the creatures and ghosts that kept sailors away from the Isle of Demons.

As time passed she became an expert hunter. One day she killed three bears herself. Their furs provided much needed warmth against the winter. Marguerite also soon discovered a source of happiness among the misery of their marooning. She was pregnant.

The joy she felt from the thought of being a mother was, like everything else that had been good in her life, short-lived. When Marguerite was near term, Etienne drank contaminated water, became ill and died. With a heavy heart, Marguerite buried him as deep as she could. But the creatures and wild animals came that night for his body. She took up a post and fended them off. It was an exhausting, frightening and stressful task she'd have to repeat night after night.

Soon her baby was born, a healthy boy that Marguerite baptized. She had little time to celebrate or relax. She took up Etienne's rifle and sword and became a warrior, fighting back against the creatures who doubled their frenzied attacks after the baby was born.

Sixteen months after being marooned, Damienne

died. Shortly thereafter, the unthinkable happened: the baby followed the same path as the servant woman and Etienne. Marguerite was alone with her grief. The creatures seemed to sense her mental weakness and increased their assaults once again, even launching attacks during the day. Marguerite dropped her face into her palms to cry and pray, but between her fingers she could see the beasts dancing around her. Her gunpowder was ruined by dampness and age and she was left with Etienne's dull sword as her last line of defence. She now had three graves to protect.

Fortunately her luck was about to turn. In the fall of 1544, more than two years after her uncle had left her on the Isle of Demons to die, ships commandeered by cod fishermen from Brittany appeared on the horizon. Marguerite called to them from the shore. Although they did not initially believe she was human, they sailed closer for a better look and realized she was not one of the fabled creatures known to inhabit the island. A team of men came ashore and Marguerite was grateful for their arrival. She showed them where she had lived and shared her sad story, and the men could scarcely believe this young, small, wild-looking woman had survived for so long in those conditions. After packing her few meagre but prized possessions, including Etienne's zither, she erected a cross before the three graves she had guarded so fiercely. Stepping foot on one of the fishermen's boats was an out-of-body experience, and as she watched the Isle of Demons fade away Marguerite was suddenly overcome by sorrow and the madness of what she had endured. She tried to jump off the ship and swim back to the island to die with those she held so dear. The fishermen restrained her before she could act so rashly and, setting aside their

Sixteenth-century map showing the Isle of Demons, or ISOLA DE DEMONI *in Italian*

work in order to take her straight back to France, set out east across the Atlantic.

Back in her home country, Marguerite became a school-mistress and never sought justice against her uncle, who died during a riot some years later. She devoted the rest of her life to shaping young minds and spreading the Word of God, sharing her courageous and remarkable story as an example of His mercy.

Once Marguerite's tale became widely known, the Isle of Demons, and the surrounding islands, were renamed the Îles de la Demoiselle in her honour. But don't let the name fool you. Fishermen today still report hearing unearthly howls carried on the wind from the island and have seen two ghosts walking its shores: a man playing a zither and a young woman dressed in bear skins, forever defending themselves from the evil creatures and apparitions that lurk in the woods.

The island may no longer be so demonic in name, but it certainly is in spirit.

STEP INTO THE COLD

Montreal, Quebec

Built in 1725, La Maison Pierre du Calvet is the oldest historical house in Montreal that now operates as a hotel. Stepping into the stone building is like stepping through a gateway that transports you three hundred years in the past. Below your feet, Moroccan rugs from wall to wall. Above your head, blood-red beamed ceilings. All around you, antique furniture, wall tapestries, crackling fireplaces and swaths of velvet and satin framing the shuttered casement windows. Behind your back, shadows skulking in the dark.

The Pierre du Calvet looks like a medieval castle, and like all true castles, it's haunted by the past. Some guests have learned that the hard way.

Enchanted by its elegant beauty and decor, one woman

checked in for five nights. The concierge assigned her to Room 3 and wished her a pleasant night. But that night would be anything but pleasant.

Early the next morning, the woman returned to the front desk. Her hair was disheveled, dark rings lined her eyes and she dragged her packed suitcase across the floor behind her. She looked like she hadn't slept a wink. Turns out, she hadn't.

When the concierge asked how he could help her, the woman replied that he could check her out of the hotel, then and there. She would not be spending one more night in the Pierre du Calvet.

When asked what was the matter with her room, the woman replied that it wasn't the room per se that was the trouble, but rather, the spirit haunting it. A woman in an old-fashioned dress had spent the entire night sitting on the bed beside her. The guest was too terrified to move and didn't dare fall asleep for fear of what might happen if she let her guard down. The ghost didn't say anything threatening and didn't touch her, but she had an evil air about her, like she resented the intrusion of the living guest in the room. Like she was coldly calculating what she should do.

La Maison Pierre du Calvet's namesake and previous owner was born in France and sailed to Quebec in 1758 to become a merchant in the new world, but he lost all of his merchandise in a shipwreck upon his arrival. As great a setback as that accident was, it was significantly less tragic than a second shipwreck, in 1786, which claimed Pierre du Calvet's life at sea. Between shipwrecks, du Calvet worked hard to re-establish his inventory and become a storekeeper, was appointed as justice of the peace for Montreal and, as a notorious sympathizer of the American Revolution, welcomed Benjamin Franklin and countless other famous guests to his home. He led an active, busy life but he also found time to start a family when he married Marie-Louise Jussaume in October 1773. Together they had three sons, but only one survived. Their marriage, similarly, was destined not to last. Marie-Louise died three years after their wedding. The cause of her death is mysterious and unknown, the hallmarks of a restless spirit with unfinished business.

Rumours swirled around Montreal claiming that Marie-Louise got along well — too well — with her husband's male guests who stayed overnight in their home. These accusations found their way to du Calvet's ear and infected his mind like maggots wriggling in his brain. Some believe that his jealousy blackened his soul and in a fit of rage he murdered his young wife for her accused sins. He was never charged for playing any part in Marie-Louise's death, however, and the truth was lost when a Spanish ship, sailing from New York to England, sank during a violent gale, claiming the lives of du Calvet and everyone else on board.

These days, Marie-Louise remains in her former home, keeping one eye on the female guests and the other on the males. Men staying in the hotel have seen her ghost step from the shadows to smile at them with a wink, while Marie-Louise gives women the literal cold shoulder. Or, in the case of Kat, a woman from New York who spent a night in 2013, a cold hand. Early in the morning while lying in bed, Kat was awoken when the ghost appeared and grabbed her arm. Kat was unable to move, open her eyes or even scream out in terror. For some inexplicable reason, she was forced to lie as still as a statue throughout the terrifying ordeal. After an uncertain length of time, Kat was finally able to kick her legs and break free from the ghost's grasp. She opened her eyes, but Marie-Louise had disappeared.

The staff at the hotel have also witnessed bizarre things and felt an angry presence in the rooms and halls. One day, a maid finished making a bed and stepped out of the room for a moment. When she returned, the sheets that had been pulled tight and tucked under the mattress were ruffled and there was an indent as if someone was lying in the middle of the bed.

A man who worked in the hotel's restaurant felt Marie-Louise's presence on nights when he was cleaning alone. At first the spirit seemed pleasant enough and he tried to ignore it, unaware that he did so at his own peril. For the ghost demanded attention, and he began to feel that her presence was becoming menacing. Eventually the unseen company of the ghost became too oppressive for him to carry on with his closing duties, so he screamed at the top of his lungs for her to go away and leave him alone. Apparently Marie-Louise finally got the message and backed off, leaving him in peace from that day forward.

On the main floor is a greenhouse conservatory that is home to many exotic birds, including two parrots named Pedro and Chico. These two characters enjoy the company of both hotel staff and guests, and welcome everyone who enters the room with a chipper *"Allô, allô!"* Their greeting is a friendly sound that never fails to warm the hearts of those who hear it. Except, of course, when the room is empty and Pedro and Chico can be heard welcoming someone unseen into their greenhouse. It's believed animals are more highly attuned to the spirits of the departed, and the hotel's employees make sure to give the greenhouse a wide berth when they hear the parrots talking to an empty room.

Maison Pierre du Calvet

It seems the hotel's owners aren't merely being poetic when they issue the following welcome to prospective guests:

> *Take root for a few days*
> *Be filled with wonder*
> *Take part in our history*

How much history you wish to take part in is entirely up to you.

RED AS BLOOD

Vancouver, British Columbia

They'd had a long flight and the young couple visiting from Japan were eager to check into the Fairmont Hotel Vancouver. Little did they know that the floor their room was located on — the fourteenth — is known to be a hot-bed of paranormal activity.

Nothing seemed amiss as they exited the elevator and walked to their room. They unlocked the door and stepped inside, ready to crawl into bed and sleep off their jetlag. But much to their surprise the room was already occupied. There was a lady in a luxurious red dress sitting on the edge of the bed. She said nothing and made no action to leave. She just sat. And stared.

Assuming an innocent mistake had been made and the room was double-booked, the husband and wife apologized and backed out of the room. They went to the front desk and reported what had happened, but hotel staff could find no record of anyone else being checked into the same room.

"What did this woman look like?" the hotel employee asked.

The couple described a beautiful young woman in her twenties wearing a bright red dress, red as blood. She appeared ready for a fancy ball.

That was exactly what the employee expected to hear. The woman in the couple's room was no living guest, but a ghost — the Hotel Vancouver's infamous Lady in Red.

After a series of stalled attempts to complete its construction, the Hotel Vancouver (affectionately known as the Hotel Van) was finally completed and open to the public in 1939. It was a time of excitement and prosperity. The Great Depression was over and the city of Vancouver was abuzz. The official opening of the chateau-style hotel was attended by Britain's King George VI and Queen Elizabeth, and the first of many Christmas balls was held by year's end in the elegant Pacific Ballroom. Brightly lit and decorated pine trees filled the interior of the hotel, while imposing, Gothic gargoyles stood guard on the copper roof outside. The Hotel Van's annual Christmas ball became a staple of the season, beloved by the city's well-to-do citizens, but the party — and indeed, the very hotel itself — was adored by no one more than Jennie Pearl Cox.

With her husband, Harold, and their six-year-old daughter, Dottie, Jennie strode into the Hotel Van's lobby for the inaugural Christmas ball and immediately fell in love. The family checked into a room, and Harold and Dottie dressed in their finest. But their breath was stolen when they laid eyes on Jennie in her stunning red dress. It

Fairmont Hotel Vancouver

was a dress so perfectly suited both for the season and for Jennie that she wore it to each Christmas ball for the next four years. In fact, she's decided to wear it for eternity.

In the summer of 1944, Jennie, Harold and Dottie were returning to the city from a relaxing countryside picnic. The sun glistened in the city's windows under a brilliant blue sky. The tragedy that was barreling toward the happy family in the form of a delivery truck was a complete contradiction to their moods. The truck rounded a corner, and Harold saw it too late. It struck their car with a sickening crunch. Metal squealed and glass shattered. There were no survivors. Coincidentally, Jennie and her family died on the street in front of her favourite place in the world, the hotel where they had celebrated Christmas for the past five years.

Following her far-too-early death, it gradually became apparent that Jennie couldn't bring herself to leave the hotel behind. She is regularly seen in her red dress gliding along the fourteenth floor. She's even been spotted floating outside on ledges, gazing longingly at the city she loved so much. And the Japanese couple who walked in on her aren't the only people who have found her spending her afterlife haunting the hotel's rooms. Eugene Mensch, Hotel Van's bell captain, recalls the time one of his staff escorted some guests to room 1403. The people entered the room quickly and the door swung shut behind them, leaving the bellman alone in the hallway — or so he thought. Suddenly, the Lady in Red flew toward the bellman and passed straight through the door. He hurried inside to warn the guests, but they were alone in the room. Jennie had vanished.

Many movies and television shows have filmed scenes in the Hotel Van, including *The X-Files*. The hotel's period charm perfectly suited the show's supernatural plot-line and dark atmosphere. But had the production team known about the real ghost haunting its halls they might have thought twice about filming there. A crew member working on the show in the '90s was setting up film equipment on the fourteenth floor when he was confronted by The Lady in Red. Leaving his equipment behind, he immediately vacated the hotel and refused to return to work there. Some believe that Jennie, who was an amateur stage actress, was curious about the production of the show.

As terrifying as those sightings have been, the creepiest experiences have taken place in and around the hotel's elevators. When the hotel was constructed in the '30s, not all of the shafts had elevators installed. There is a dummy shaft that only has doors on the first and fourteenth floors. These doors are bolted shut from the inside for safety, making them impossible to open. That hasn't stopped The Lady in Red. Mensch has reported that both a bellman and an assistant manager have seen the bolted doors open on their own, and it's not uncommon for people to see Jennie float in and out of the unfinished elevator. It's as if she's using it as her own personal elevator to and from her favourite floor.

More recently, security cameras have detected unusual activity in one of the stairwells near the fourteenth floor. A staff member, who prefers to remain anonymous, reports that video footage confirms the existence of a ghost in the Hotel Van. The camera turns on automatically when someone passes in front of it, a security measure to alert the guards if someone tries to gain unauthorized access to the roof. Late one night the camera turned on but no one could be seen in the stairwell. However, the sound of footsteps could be heard slowly climbing the stairs toward the camera. Once the sound was at its loudest, an odd shadow passed before the camera and then, shortly thereafter, a disembodied shriek filled the stairwell.

The Lady in Red's afterlife activity has gained her a great deal of fame. Not only are spooky stories shared amongst employees and the many guests who have witnessed unexplainable events over the years, but the hotel's bar has honoured her presence by naming a drink after her. And so, Jennie Pearl Cox has gained a certain amount of immortality in her beloved hotel. There's little doubt she would approve.

STAGE FRIGHT

Edmonton, Alberta

As if the stress of performing live on stage in front of an audience of 145 people weren't enough to deal with, a ghost has been disturbing actors in the Walterdale Theatre for years. Stage hands say not a week goes by without some sort of paranormal activity being reported in the theatre. Most members of the theatre group try to ignore the unexplainable sights, sounds and sensations, particularly during performances, but that's not always possible. Sometimes, the ghost tries his best to stop the show from going on.

One night an actor was getting ready in the second-floor dressing room before taking the stage. No one else was with her. She slipped into her costume and applied makeup while going over her lines. She stood and turned her back to the dressing table for just a moment, but that was enough time for the theatre's ghost to act. The woman returned to the table only to discover her wig had been taken. A quick search of the dressing room turned up nothing. That's when panic set in. She needed the wig and was due on stage in thirty minutes. She ran around the theatre rounding up everyone who could help. They searched every square inch of the building. Finally, just moments before the curtain was set to rise, the wig was found on the main floor near a pile of stage props. Although the actor was relieved, no one could say how the wig had gotten there.

That hair-raising experience is just one of the many times the ghost, nicknamed Walter after the theatre he haunts, has interfered with a show. It's believed that he's the spirit of a volunteer firefighter who died in 1909 while the building was being constructed. The building was originally home to the oldest fire hall in Alberta. The fire hall was in operation until 1954 when it became a furniture warehouse, followed by the Walterdale Theatre in 1974. Since that time the theatre has become a major part of Edmonton's thriving arts and culture scene despite Walter's presence.

He's often seen floating through the theatre's halls, dressing rooms and stairwell. He's fond of moving important props and costumes, like the runaway wig, when they're needed most. Lights flicker and cold spots envelop theatre-goers. The piano occasionally plays itself and people have heard the Tower Bell ring loudly without anyone near it. As if that wasn't enough, Walter is also known to walk loudly throughout the building at inopportune times.

Richard Hatfield, the theatre group's technical director, recalls the time that Walter tried his best to interrupt

Walterdale Theatre

a show. Along with a few other crew members, Hatfield was in the theatre's sound booth on the main floor. All was going well until they heard footfalls directly above their heads, loud enough that Hatfield feared the audience would be distracted by the noise. He immediately called the crew that were upstairs and told them to stop clomping around. Their response was unsettling to say the least. No one on the second floor had moved in a long, long time. They'd all been still throughout the performance. In order to calm the crew and not create any fear, Hatfield brushed the phantom footfalls off and tried to convince the others that it might have been crew members on the main floor that they heard. But even as he said it, he knew it couldn't be true. The main floor was made of concrete — a surface that wouldn't produce the hollow *thud-clomp-thud-clomp* they had heard — and everyone agreed the footfalls had definitely come from above. Distressingly, this wasn't an isolated incident. Hatfield has to work late from time to time, and often alone. Or so he would like to believe. Sometimes, when the theatre is dark and quiet, he suddenly hears the same heavy feet stomping across the floor above. He stops what he's doing and rushes upstairs to investigate, but all he ever finds is an empty room. The place is quite dead.

Dead, maybe. But silent? Not in the Walterdale Theatre.

THE WATCHER IN THE NIGHT

O'Leary, Prince Edward Island

On a clear day from the top of the West Point lighthouse you can see New Brunswick across the turbulent waters of the Northumberland Strait. At a height of 20.62 metres, it's the tallest lighthouse in the province. Amazingly, only two keepers tended the lighthouse's fire during the eighty-eight years before it became electric in 1963: William "Willie" Anderson MacDonald, the first keeper from 1875 to 1925, and Benjamin MacIsaac, who was keeper from 1925 to 1963. The lighthouse had to be lit each and every day, and it's said that Willie didn't miss a single one during his tenure, not for sickness or vacation. Not even death can keep him away.

In 1984 the lighthouse was converted to include an inn, restaurant and museum. For the first few years in operation, volunteers spent two nights a week in the lighthouse to give the manager time off. If there were no guests in the inn by nine o'clock, the volunteer would lock the inn and go home. One summer evening, once the restaurant had closed and staff had gone home, Merna Boulter, the volunteer on duty, waited patiently as the clock slowly ticked away the time. Finally, once it was nine and not a soul was around, Merna prepared to leave.

She climbed the seventy-two stairs to the top of the lighthouse, making sure all was well. Nothing seemed out of the ordinary and the only sound that accompanied her footsteps was the crashing of waves on the beach outside. After turning off the lights and locking the door behind her, Merna got in her car.

That's odd, she thought. There was a light coming from a bedroom above the lighthouse's veranda. *That wasn't on a moment before . . .*

There was nothing to do but go back inside to investigate. She climbed the stairs and entered the lit room. It was still empty. No sounds, nothing stirring. With a final, hesitant scan of the room, Merna turned the light off and left the lighthouse once again, this time a little quicker.

After locking the door and walking to her car, she couldn't resist stealing another glance over her shoulder. Merna stopped dead. The light had been turned back on.

There was no chance Merna was going to risk her well-being by going back into the lighthouse alone that night. She left without hesitation, saying that whatever presence wanted the light that badly could keep it on.

That wasn't the last time the lights suggested that the living weren't the only people dwelling in the lighthouse. A few years later, a group of volunteers had been going over an architect's renovation plans before calling it a night.

They had been instructed to turn off all the switches in the main control panel, except for the one that controlled the navigation light, before locking up. They ensured the building was empty, turned out the lights and then shut off the power at the control panel. But just before they left, someone remembered the architect's drawings were still in the kitchen. Because the building was shrouded in darkness, the volunteer who went in needed a flashlight to see. After retrieving the drawings, the volunteer passed the flashlight's beam over the kitchen for a final check — all was well — and hastened to rejoin the others.

As they drove home, their car was stopped by a person who informed them that a distraught neighbour was missing. It was feared that this person might try to enter the lighthouse, climb to the top and jump to his death. Although they had locked the door, they decided it would be best to return to the lighthouse and double-check that the man had not found a way in.

Fortunately, the suicidal man was found elsewhere, safe and sound, but how could the volunteers explain what they encountered back at the lighthouse? After unlocking the door and stepping tentatively inside, they discovered that the kitchen light had been turned on. It made no sense. The control panel's switches were still turned off, so the lights were receiving no power. There was only one explanation that anyone could fathom. Willie was in the building.

In the years since these events, many guests have reported that the bedroom's lights turned on when no one else was around. With a laugh, staff reveal that it's just the ghost of Willie playing tricks with the light. Having served as keeper for fifty years, working the lights is in his flesh and blood — figuratively speaking, of course.

Willian Anderson MacDonald

THE ARTIST NEVER DIES

Victoria, British Columbia

Most of the staff at the James Bay Inn work with one eye on their task and one eye on the dark corners in each of the hotel's guestrooms. Camiel, who admits that working alone in the hotel is very creepy, has experienced many scary events since she began working there as a housekeeper and at the front desk. One day she was meeting with her boss, Steve, in his small office. Steve left for a moment to get something and Camiel thought she was alone. She wasn't. The silver bell on the front desk outside the office suddenly rang. The ding was a familiar sound alerting staff that a customer was waiting for service, but Camiel could see the front desk. She could see the bell. No one was standing anywhere near it.

Ding! The bell rang again.

Camiel stood, left the office, scanned the front of the hotel to ensure there wasn't anyone hiding anywhere and then examined the bell. There was no way it could ring on its own. But somehow it had. Camiel felt that something was trying to get her attention, but the spirit's intent remained a mystery.

The next time one of the hotel's ghosts tried to get her attention, its intentions were abundantly clearer. A month after the bell rang, Camiel and another employee, Jasmine, were cleaning the bar early in the morning before it was open. Once again, Camiel thought she and her co-worker were alone. Once again, she was wrong.

The two cleaned while listening to hip hop on the radio. The music made the monotonous chore a little more bearable, but suddenly the radio switched to a Christian rock station. With a shrug of the shoulders, Camiel and Jasmine crossed the room and turned the radio back to the hip-hop station. They returned to their work, but the radio soon switched stations again, this time to jazz music. The two women exchanged a nervous glance. They were starting to get freaked out. They slowly approached the radio and changed back to the hip-hop station once more, and the radio immediately turned off. Dead silence filled the bar. Without a word both Camiel and Jasmine knew what to do. They ran.

It's common knowledge there's a ghost haunting the hotel, a ghost that's eager to ensnare the souls of anyone who dares to criticize the artwork of Emily Carr, one of Canada's most famous painters. That's because the ghost is Carr herself, who died in the building in 1945. Locals and tourists who gather in the James Bay Inn's pub and restaurant enjoy lively discussions about Carr, an eccentric artist who painted forest landscapes and First

Nations villages and imagery of the Pacific Northwest Coast, but they're careful not to be too critical of her work. Those who know better are fearful of Carr's curse. Say the wrong thing about one of her paintings and you might find yourself trapped in the James Bay Inn for an eternity.

The hotel, which opened in 1911, had a brief interlude as a hospital run by Mother Cecilia's religious order from 1942 to 1945. It was during this time that Carr was admitted due to

Emily Carr

health complications and spent her final days. She passed her time painting in the upstairs lobby and then took her art outside to sell on the street corner. She died in her room from a heart attack, one of many that she suffered late in her life.

Shortly after the priory turned back into a hotel, Carr's ghost began appearing in guests' bedrooms late at night. Startled customers have been awoken by televisions that have turned themselves on with the volume raised to ear-splitting levels. Others have received telephone calls without anyone on the other end and no record of incoming calls. Lights flicker, and a gas fireplace on one of the upper floors turns itself on when it gets too cold, even for a ghost.

As active as she is in and around the guestrooms, Carr is most often seen in the pub and restaurant. That time Camiel's hip-hop music kept changing? She believes Carr was to blame, that she didn't approve of Camiel's music selection. Now whenever Camiel enters the bar area at night she calls out, "Hi, Emmie, it's just me."

That doesn't stop Carr's ghost from scaring staff by opening doors and rattling the restaurant's dishes. She once reached out and grabbed a bartender's leg from behind, then squeezed him tightly, painfully, causing him to shout out and startle the other people in the bar.

Perhaps she's upset with the new use of the bedroom in which she passed away. During renovations the room was converted into the men's bathroom. Guests often feel like they've walked through an intense cold spot when they enter the bathroom and then feel as if they're being watched while going about their business.

Some say her ghost is so protective of her legacy that she'll not only turn on dissenters but curse them to return to the hotel following their own deaths, forever trapping them in the haunted hotel with Carr herself.

If you're not a fan of Carr's art, you'd better be careful what you say in the the James Bay Inn.

THE DOCTOR WILL SEE YOU NOW

Collingwood, Ontario

Have you ever entered an old building or room alone and immediately known that something bad had happened there? Your head starts to spin, your stomach suddenly drops and your skin breaks out in a cold sweat. You feel as if you're not as alone as you had thought, nor as you had hoped.

That happened to three professional women in their mid-forties from Ottawa who shared a three-room suite in the Beild House Country Inn & Spa in September 2014. As soon as they entered their room for the first time, two of the three friends felt a weird energy that they tried — and failed — to shake off. While they played board games and had a late-afternoon snack, one of the friends kept seeing an odd presence in the hallway of their suite. They left the inn and ventured into town for the night, returning well after midnight and quickly settling into bed. Two of the friends shared one of the bedrooms, but they weren't about to get any sleep. Things, they recall with unease, were about to get really weird.

As soon as they laid down, they felt on edge, restless, anxious, uneasy and unsettled. Waves of inexplicable nausea washed over them as if something in the air was making them ill. Then they started to hear things. It wasn't a bump in the night — more of a rattle and shake, and the sound was unnervingly relentless. They thought it might be passing trucks, but the sound never faded. Perhaps it was a rodent in the walls, but it wasn't a scurrying sound, and it was growing louder.

At their wits' end, the friends scanned the room and finally located the source of the sound — a revelation that still sends shivers up their spines. Their attention was drawn to two porcelain plates on the wall at the head of the bed. Something was rattling them violently, as if the weird energy they had felt in the room was trying to shake the plates loose. They sat up in bed, scared and confused. One of the women shouted, "Take them down!" The other removed them from the wall and placed them on the bedside table, where the plates slowly and quietly stopped shaking. But the room didn't remain silent for long.

They soon heard a muffled conversation, an unusual whispering, somehow coming from the air all around them. And the temperature plummeted to bone-chilling, teeth-chattering lows.

When the sun finally rose the next morning, they hurried to leave without showering. And who can blame them? It was clear that one of the Beild House's ghosts was to blame. Was it simply a bit of harmless fun, or do the spirits that occupy the turn-of-the-century home harbour a hidden, malicious intent?

Construction of the house began in 1909 but took three years. It was built for Dr. Joseph Robbins Arthur, who opened an office and consulting rooms in the north part of the home. He lived with his wife, daughter and son in the living quarters, which faced south to the garden. Dr. Arthur chose the name *Beild* for the Scottish word for "shelter." And a grand shelter it was; the good doctor opened his home to transients passing through town during the Great Depression, giving them a hot meal and new clothing.

The home also sheltered Dr. Arthur's father-in-law, Henry Robertson, in his latter years, as well as Dr. Arthur's daughter, Bethia, who also spent her final years on the third floor where she had fond childhood memories of playing with the gymnastics rings her father had installed there.

The question remains: who haunts the Beild House today? There are many theories. The prime suspect is Dr. Arthur himself, a fashionable dresser who some cleaning staff have reported seeing in the guestrooms. Two sisters-in-law from England, both mediums who can communicate with the dead, stayed in the inn one night and communicated with Dr. Arthur's spirit. They discovered that he was confused and didn't know where to go after he died, so he returned to his home. Perhaps he'll never find closure and will remain in the Beild House until the end of time.

As innocent as his intentions may be, Dr. Arthur's sudden appearance in the night remains a haunting vision that terrifies people staying there. Even owner Bill Barclay, who regularly hears from guests who have experienced paranormal activity, has seen Dr. Arthur's ghost. He awoke once to see a man in a top hat standing under the archway of his bedroom. Once the ghost was spotted, he silently receded into the shadows and was gone, leaving Barclay feeling very conflicted, to say the least.

Although the doctor might be stuck in limbo, at least he has company. The English sisters-in-law also identified a second spirit dwelling in the inn. Spending her afterlife with Dr. Arthur is Barclay's great-grandmother, a small but powerful woman who is following Dr. Arthur around to make sure he behaves.

Beild House

It's also believed that daughter Bethia is so fond of the Beild House's attic that she remains on the third floor, walking around and waking guests with the sound of foot-steps in the middle of the night. One guest was awoken by a creepier sound that made it difficult to fall back asleep: cackling laughter.

If you faint at the sight of blood, you'll especially want to avoid the final ghost who has been seen in the Beild House. Known as Head Wound Lady, this disturbing apparition has been reported by many guests over the years. Returning from a long day and ready for a good night's sleep, people have been passed by a woman quickly running downstairs in blood-stained clothing. The blood on her clothes is gushing from a fresh cut on her head. Once their shock fades, the alarmed guests run to the front desk to report what they've seen. Employees search the building and check on the other guests, but no one is ever found to be injured. The bleeding ghost has disappeared. Some believe her to be the doctor's late wife. Whoever the ghost is, at least she's spending her afterlife in the same building as a man who might be able to tend to her wound.

Spend a night in the Beild House Country Inn & Spa and the doctor will see you, whether you want him to or not.

ROOM 473

St. Andrews by-the-Sea, New Brunswick

After a long day showing people around St. Andrews by-the-Sea, a tour leader made sure everyone was settled in their rooms at the Algonquin Resort and then slipped into her own. She didn't get the rest she needed, however, as her sleep was disturbed by the loud and sorrowful weeping of a woman in room 473, directly beside her own. This went on for some time without abating, and the woman grew concerned for the guest next door, who she assumed was part of her tour group. She called the front desk and reported it, hoping someone could check on the woman to make sure she was okay. But the crying carried on through the night. The next morning the tour guide asked front desk staff if the woman in room 473 was all right, but the employee had some alarming news. No one had been checked into that room — it had been empty all night.

No one who worked at the Algonquin was surprised. They knew the tour guide's sleep had been broken by the ghost bride who haunts room 473. She's been seen in her wedding dress by many guests and staff members over the years, such as a cleaning lady who had finished tidying the infamous room. When she looked up, the ghost bride was seated in a chair. The cleaning lady froze. The ghost bride nodded with a wan smile on her face. Without any further hesitation, the cleaning lady promptly turned and left, making double sure to close the door tightly behind her.

It's believed that sometime in the early 1900s a young local woman was engaged to a wealthy American. Their wedding ceremony was to be held in a St. Andrews by-the-Sea church, followed by a honeymoon at the Algonquin. The bride checked into room — you guessed it — 473 and excitedly prepared for the ceremony. With butterflies in her stomach she did her makeup and hair, then slipped into her beautiful white wedding dress. Ready to start her new life with her husband-to-be, she left the hotel and arrived at the church.

She waited. And waited. Then waited some more. The groom was late. At first she assumed he was simply running a little behind. As more time passed she grew concerned that some accident had delayed him. Finally the bride was informed that the groom would not be coming. He had developed cold feet about the union and decided to back out.

Devastated, the bride raced back to the seclusion of her hotel room. She didn't want to be around anyone. But hiding in the room where she was supposed to spend her honeymoon did nothing to improve her state of mind. Other guests staying nearby complained about the sound of her cries — which alternated between sad and angry — and the hotel staff monitored the situation. Wishing there was something they could do to relieve the young woman of her misery, they sat and waited, listening to her sobs . . . until she suddenly stopped.

They were hopeful she had gotten over the worst of her grief and fallen asleep. Unfortunately, the situation had taken a darker turn. The bride was found outside, her broken body lying motionless on the ground below her open window four storeys above. Bright red blood soaked into her wedding dress, a stark contrast to the white fabric and lace. The pain of her fiancé's rejection was too great a burden to bear, and she decided to end her own life rather than face another day of heartache.

Elaine Bruff, a St. Andrews by-the-Sea resident who leads a seasonal haunted walk through town, has tried to find any information that could reveal who the bride was, but her searches have come up empty. It's her belief that the groom's rich and powerful family used their considerable wealth to keep the suicide hush-hush in order to maintain their reputation. It's Elaine's hope that if the ghost bride could be identified, she'd find some peace and be able to move on.

For the time being, the mystery remains, as does the midnight wailing heard in room 473.

THE NiGHT SHiFT

Winnipeg, Manitoba

For twenty-seven years, Ben, a security guard who worked the night shift in the Manitoba Legislative Building, never felt comfortable in one of the second floor offices. It was one of those hard-to-put-your-finger-on kind of feelings. Although it defied explanation, Ben described a general sense that he was out of place. Unwelcome. Unwanted.

Late one evening, Ben found out why. Several mediums who were visiting the building, nicknamed "The Ledge," gave him some unsettling news. The office was home to the ghosts of three old men who meet every night once the building has closed. And the ghosts weren't happy with Ben's nightly rounds — they informed the mediums that the frequent interruptions were a nuisance. The spirits demanded that Ben knock on the door before entering.

From that night on, Ben was happy to oblige the ghosts. He knocked on the office door. And the odd, hard-to-explain feeling he felt inside the office? Gone.

There is only one confirmed death to have occurred in the building. In 1947 Deputy Treasury Minister Ralph McNeil Pearson shot himself in his office. The circumstances of the suicide are mysterious and no one knows why he took his own life. But before you arrive at the conclusion that Pearson must be the sole source of the paranormal activity in the Ledge, remember there are *three* ghosts who meet nightly after hours. And even they aren't alone.

Like Ben, most of the security guards who work the night shift have come face to face with a host of spectres. There's a woman who glides through the basement's halls. With a quiet voice as gentle and smooth as silk she sings lullabies of years long past.

An elderly gentleman in a top hat and tails takes nighttime strolls throughout the second floor and has been spotted walking up and down the thirteen steps of the grand staircase. When confronted he flies straight through the nearest stone wall.

One guard was surprised when she turned a corner and found a person staring back at her. At first she mistook the figure for an intruder, but then, with a sickening feeling in her gut that caused the hairs on the back of her neck to stand on end, she realized she was in the presence of a ghost. She considered hitting the alarm, but at that moment the apparition disappeared before her eyes.

Yet another guard was terribly startled when he saw two boys in the basement. They pressed their hands and faces up to a frosted window pane of a meeting room, their silhouettes more shadow-looking than real. The guard couldn't understand how the boys had gotten into the

Inside the Manitoba Legislative Building

building nor what they were doing there in the middle of the night, so he barged into the room and demanded an explanation for their presence. But the room, he discovered, was empty.

And then there's the phantom librarian. Although no one knows who she was in life, her ghost is well known to the guards and library staff. Many have seen her, and although she has never hurt anyone, no one has any desire to see her again. Clad in a long flowing dress in the style of the early 1900s, she floats from room to room on the upper floor. She's an old woman with grey hair tied in a bun and she never makes a sound. Seemingly unaware of the living around her, she stacks books on shelves with grim determination. But even the dead need to take work breaks. Once, a security guard unlocked a door and entered a room. There, sitting at a table reading a book, was the librarian. Not realizing at first that she was the infamous ghost his colleagues had reported seeing, he asked how she had entered a locked room.

The librarian felt no need to answer the guard's question. This was, after all, her place of work. True to form, she disappeared without a sound.

If you visit the Manitoba Legislative Building during the night, you're sure to see visions from beyond the grave. In fact, it's best to avoid the building altogether after sunset. Unfortunately for the guards who work the night shift, that's not an option.

THE CURSED CASTLE

Victoria, British Columbia

There's something about the Dunsmuirs. It seems many members of this famous family just don't want to stay dead.

Fit for a king, Craigdarroch Castle was home to the man who was not-so-affectionately known as "King Grab." Robert Dunsmuir was regarded as a greedy entrepreneur by much of the province, who believed he had achieved his success by any means possible, including paying off politicians and taking advantage of the working class.

In 1887 construction of Craigdarroch Castle began. Spread out over four floors, there are thirty-nine rooms within, each one more dazzling than the last. At the top of the grand staircase is a ballroom that Dunsmuir had built to entertain the social elite and, he hoped, result in the marriage of his three daughters. It was a grand plan for a grand home, but Dunsmuir would not be afforded the luxury of seeing it through to the end. He died in 1889 at the age of sixty-three, one year before the house was completed. An air of mystery surrounded his death, as Dunsmuir was thought to be in perfect health before contracting a cold that, four days later, sent him into a coma and, two days after that, claimed his life. No one could say Dunsmuir had left this Earth without unfinished business. He — or rather, his ghost — can hardly be blamed for wanting to stick around.

The Dunsmuir family was beset by further tragedies and hardships over the years. Craigdarroch's original architect, Warren Heywood Williams, died of an enlarged heart before seeing his grandest project through to completion. In 1889 the second Dunsmuir daughter, Agnes, died of typhoid fever and her husband, John Harvey, died of the same disease shortly after. Their orphaned children moved into the castle once it was completed along with their widowed grandmother, Joan, and her three still-unmarried daughters. Moving into Craigdarroch should have been a happy occasion filled with celebration, but instead the mood was dour and bleak. Too many had died unexpectedly in a short period. For the Dunsmuirs, it was a time plagued by grief. Some said the castle was cursed.

Slowly, as the passage of time healed their wounds, the family began to enjoy their beautiful home. It was the setting of many lavish parties, but there was one final nail waiting to be hammered into the Dunsmuir family's coffin. In 1908, Joan Dunsmuir passed away. The castle was too expensive for any of her surviving children to maintain and it had to be sold, its contents auctioned to the highest bidder.

Craigdarroch Castle

The mansion passed through many hands until 1979 when the Castle Society, a group dedicated to preserving Craigdarroch's history and operating it as a museum, took possession and began restoring the building to its former glory.

One afternoon during restorations, a worker took a much needed break by the grand staircase. He sat in a comfortable chair after lunch and allowed his mind to wander but nearly toppled over when he looked at the stairs. Gliding down the staircase was a woman's foot in a satin shoe beneath a beautiful gown that flowed down the steps behind her. The foot descended the stairs as if in slow motion but no other foot ever appeared, nor did the rest of the woman.

In 2011 a Californian family of six travelled to British

Columbia and visited the castle. They split up inside. Standing before a closed door, the clan's matriarch, Lupe, bumped into her son-in-law, Dan, and they decided to enter the room together. Little did they know what lay in wait for them.

On the far side of the room, standing all alone, was her husband, Alan. He looked shaken and strange. Lupe and Dan didn't know why, but they knew something was wrong. Behind Alan was a staircase partially hidden by a wall that concealed the upper steps. Suddenly, Lupe saw something that left her feeling shaken: a pair of legs walking up the stairs and out of sight.

"Who was that?" she asked, a slight tremor in her voice. She didn't think any other guests were in the room with them.

Alan looked confused and concerned. He said he had been all alone in the room before his wife and son-in-law entered a moment before.

But Dan had seen the legs fly up the stairs too. "We just saw a man going up those stairs!" he told his father-in-law.

Assuming the legs must have belonged to a museum employee, Lupe led them up the creaky stairs. When they got to the top, their path was blocked by a door made from solid wood and glass. They tried to open it, but it didn't have a doorknob and, furthermore, it was bolted shut.

No living human could have passed through it.

Could there be some relation between the foot the restoration worker witnessed going downstairs and the legs Lupe saw going up? It does seem to be an odd coincidence. Visitors should make double sure to hold the handrails tightly when walking up and down between the castle's floors.

Although some of the museum's staff members official-ly deny the existence of ghosts in the castle, many have had paranormal encounters. A woman saw a maid in a Victorian-style uniform enter a room, look from side to side and then vanish on the spot. A man came face to face with three spirits while employed at the museum: a little girl haunting the basement and two soldiers who have taken root in a bedroom that was used as a hospital in the early 1900s. The man described it as a "painful" room that many people dislike entering.

Some guests haven't even gotten that far. Over the years there has been no shortage of people who have refused to enter the castle due to an overwhelming feeling of unease. Those who do stay and explore Craigdarroch have walked through intense cold spots on warm summer days, seen some of the artifacts levitate, been pushed from behind when all alone and heard the faint

Main staircase of Craigdarroch Castle

sobs of an unseen child in the halls. It's common for guests to smell the strong aroma of burning candles coming from Joan's room despite the fact that none have been lit. It's said that Joan loved aromatic candles and lit them each and every day. Perhaps she still does.

And then there's the piano. The Dunsmuir Steinway grand piano is played throughout the year during special recitals for large crowds who enjoy the old-timey jazz and beautiful Christmas melodies, but it's not only used during the museum's open hours. Once night has fallen and the castle is locked up, the piano often comes to life and plays on its own. The music is sad and haunting, and many believe Robert Dunsmuir himself is playing his beloved Steinway in the house he never had the luxury of inhabiting — except, of course, in his afterlife.

THE BOG WRAITHS

Pelly Crossing, Yukon

Deep in the heart of the Yukon, four angry men lurk in the bogs. They spend their time — and they have plenty of it — prowling this barren and bleak landscape, hiding behind gnarled shrubs and trees. They don't take kindly to intruders, particularly of the living and breathing variety. Fortunately for anyone who should inadvertently cross these men in the middle of the night, they have a fifth companion, a young girl who takes pity on travellers passing through their bog. If not for her, well, there's no telling what the men might do.

Between Whitehorse and Dawson City lies the small community of Pelly Crossing. It's an extremely cold area with average temperatures topping out at 12.7°C in August and record lows of -60°C in the winter. The land doesn't get warm enough in the summer to fully thaw and therefore it doesn't completely drain of water when the winter snow melts, absorbing it beneath a spongy surface that resembles grass instead. This creates a bogland known as muskeg that's particular to the Far North, and it can be nasty, treacherous stuff. One minute you're walking on solid ground, the next you're slogging through a seemingly endless sea of waist-deep water and muck. This bizarre, unearthly-looking landscape has been known to swallow animals as big as moose, drowning them below the surface with no chance of escape.

Even those familiar with the safest paths to tread can find themselves in peril if they're not always vigilant. Jerry, a prospector who knew the bogland well, found himself in a tricky situation one day while trekking through them. The evening was growing old; the light had faded and he couldn't see the ground he and his old dog, Max, were walking on. Suddenly he sank into the ground and had to struggle to free his feet. He tried to find a way out of the deep muskeg but every which way he turned only made things worse. Finally, just as the sunlight was completely extinguished and Jerry could barely see five feet in front of his face, he climbed a small mound of solid ground with one lonely tree growing from it for him to lean against. With some of the tree's small, weather-beaten branches he was able to build a fire to warm his hands. Max curled up in his lap and Jerry rubbed the dog's belly, happy not to be alone in the wilderness. As he sat and contemplated his next move, Jerry's eyes began to droop and he slipped into a jittery sleep.

Sometime later, Jerry was awoken by the sound of Max growling. The dog was clearly agitated by something. His teeth were bared and his stance was tense and rigid. He was looking intently at something in the dark, but what? Jerry couldn't make it out, but then he heard it.

A short distance away in the bog, their pale skin glowing in the dying firelight, stood four men and a young girl. The strangers were arguing in a language Jerry didn't recognize, but their words were laced with rage. It was clear that the men's anger was directed at Jerry, but the girl was pleading with them not to do anything rash.

Searching his pockets for a weapon and curling his fingers into fists when he found none, Jerry stood up to face the threat head-on. He didn't intend on going down without a fight. Seeing this, the men and girl quickly disappeared. Not believing what he'd seen and convinced it must've been a trick of the light, Jerry slowly sat back down. It took a long time, but he eventually fell back asleep.

It wasn't long before he was awoken once again by a familiar sound.

Grrr . . .

Max was growling at the same spot in the bog. Jerry rubbed his eyes and saw the men had returned. This time they weren't so easily spooked. The men yelled and cursed at Jerry threateningly. Not to be intimidated, not even by four angry ghosts, Jerry stood up and yelled back. Once again the men disappeared, leaving Jerry in a terrified state of confusion. He sat down warily and Max immediately began to whimper. Looking in the direction of Max's nervous stare, Jerry locked eyes with the girl, who had suddenly appeared before him. Speechless, Jerry listened as the girl spoke. She warned him that he was in a dangerous predicament and gave him detailed instructions to navigate the muskeg back to safety. Without waiting for Jerry to reply she faded away gently like smoke on a soft breeze.

When the sun rose early the next morning Jerry was

thankful to be rid of the ghosts but was still stuck in the middle of the bog. Even in full daylight he couldn't see a clear path so, with nothing to lose, he followed the girl's directions with Max close at his heels. Much to his surprise and relief, the ghost had led him true and he soon found his way back to firm ground. He would never feel truly at ease trekking through the muskeg north of Pelly Crossing again.

It's believed that the men are part of a large Serbian family who, in 1874, passed through Fort Edmonton, Alberta, on their way to the Yukon River but were never seen nor heard from again. The story fits, since part of that expedition was a teenage daughter of the same age as the ghostly girl who guided Jerry out of an early grave.

No one knows why the men are so aggressive toward people who find themselves in the bog after nightfall. One can only hope that the young girl chooses to remain with her family forever instead of abandoning them to follow her own directions out of the bog.

THE VIKING GHOST BOAT

L'Anse aux Meadows, Newfoundland and Labrador

Most ghosts are doomed to forever haunt one specific location — an old house, a cemetery, an abandoned hospital — shackled by the terrible events that occurred there long ago. But the ghosts of Leif Eriksson and the other Norse Vikings that founded a small settlement in Newfoundland in the eleventh century aren't content to drop their afterlife anchor in one place. The territory they haunt spans two continents and an ocean.

On June 3, 1981, two American tourists walked along a beach near Reykjavik, Iceland. As the sun set and the warm wind tousled their hair, they were mesmerized by the beauty of the remote land surrounded by cool, blue waves. The peaceful walk was suddenly interrupted by the harsh sounds of oars slapping the water. They scanned the ocean for the source of the sound and spotted two distinctive Viking long ships being propelled by rows of oarsmen along both sides. The ships had planked hulls and one central mast apiece, each with red and white striped sails. At the helm stood a tall, bearded man in archaic clothing with a stern, proud face. He shouted something in Norwegian and the ships disappeared from sight. The scared couple returned to town and described to their tour guide what they had seen. A little nervously, the guide told them they had just seen the Viking ghost ships that sail west from Iceland each summer and arrive in Newfoundland weeks later.

Twenty days after sightings of the Viking ghost ships are reported in Iceland, similar reports surface in northern Newfoundland at L'Anse aux Meadows, the earliest known European settlement in the New World.

After the finest catch of the summer, one fisherman stayed late in his hut preparing his fish for sale when he heard the odd sound of oars in the water outside. It was late and he thought all the other fishermen had come ashore for the day, so he peered out his window but saw nothing. Thinking his ears were playing tricks on him, he returned to his work but then heard another sound, odder yet. A battle horn trumpeted across the water, shaking the walls of his hut. He dropped what he was doing and stepped outside. A thick fog rolled across the water's surface. From the centre of the mist came the Viking long ships with their red and white sails. The man watched in fear and awe as they passed by and disappeared.

Years later a pair of young criminals heard that an old fisherman kept a secret stash of whiskey in his hut by the water. Under the cover of darkness they broke in and found what they had come to steal. But just as they laid hands on the old man's bottles, they heard the same sound of oars breaking the water followed by the battle horn. They stole tentative glances through the door and saw the Viking ships headed straight for them. Despite being tough men, they were so frightened that they left the whiskey, ran from the hut and didn't tell anyone what they had seen until years later when they heard other people share similar accounts.

Another fisherman was alone on the water when he was confronted by one of the ghost ships. It had been an exceptionally good fishing day and he decided to stay out on the water later than anyone else. But the winds suddenly picked up and dark, angry clouds covered the sky. It was time to get safely back to harbour, but when he turned his boat's motor it didn't start. The fuel tank was full and a check of the connections revealed no problems, so he couldn't understand what was wrong. As the storm approached, the man heard oars on the water and stood up to wave, hoping for rescue. The ship he saw was not at all what he had expected, but was the Viking ghost ship sailing to L'Anse aux Meadows once again. It sailed straight for him as if it meant to ram his vessel, but just before the imminent collision it sounded its battle horn and disappeared before his eyes. The fisherman felt lucky to be alive. His luck continued when he tried the engine and it started without fail.

The sightings of the Viking ghost ships are often followed by chilling screams of warriors in the woods near the abandoned Viking village. There are some who believe it's the battle cries of the ghosts of ancient Inuit, the people the Vikings called Skrælings. The two sides had many bloody clashes and the Norse, greatly outnumbered by the land's inhabitants, were eventually driven back to their homeland, never to return to present-day Canada.

One such skirmish between the two sides claimed the life of Leif's brother Thorvald, who was shot by an arrow and buried near their settlement. When Leif's other brother, Thorstein, who had not joined the others on the expedition to Vinland, heard of Thorvald's death, he was determined to bring the body back home. With a crew of twenty-five men and his wife, Gudrid, Thorstein set sail for Vinland, but he would never arrive. Bad weather forced them back ashore and then, to make matters worse, disease broke out amongst the crew early that winter. Thorstein became infected and died.

He didn't stay dead. Nor did he stay quiet.

Not long after succumbing to the illness and taking his last breath, Thorstein's corpse sat bolt upright and his

Replicas of sod houses at L'Anse aux Meadows

dead eyes flashed open. Those present jumped back in alarm, muttering oaths and curses.

Thorstein opened his mouth and three words bubbled out like a pustule erupting.

Where. . . is. . . Gudrid?

His grieving wife was summoned and she listened, terrified and silent, as Thorstein made a prophecy. He told her she would soon remarry, have children, build a church in Iceland and live a long life as a nun. Having said his piece, Thorstein fell back down. He neither stirred nor spoke again.

This is believed by scholars to be the oldest European ghost story with a connection to Newfoundland. Sometimes, dead men do tell tales.

LA DAME BLANCHE

Montmorency Falls, Quebec

As the moon rises and casts a rippling silver glow across the Montmorency River, the inhabitants of Île d'Orléans have seen a haunting figure walking through the mists of Montmorency Falls. Thin as a skeleton, pale as frost and clad in a tattered wedding dress, the waterlogged woman emerges from the depths of the river and rambles along the shore. Her wails echo across the water. That her wispy voice can be heard over the crashing falls lends credence to the locals' belief that the woman is the ghost of Mathilde Robin, dead for more than two hundred fifty years.

Whatever you do, don't get it in your head that you should rush to the woman's aid. Those who have gotten too close to the Woman in White have learned how deadly she can be.

In 1759 Mathilde Robin was the happiest girl in the Côte-de-Beaupré region. She was young and in love, and engaged to Louis Tessier, a strong and honourable farmer who adored her. While Louis worked the land, Mathilde worked in secret designing and sewing by hand the dress she'd wear on her wedding day. After a long day's work, the young couple walked hand in hand under the stars to the top of Montmorency Falls to gaze down at Île d'Orléans. Despite Louis's prodding to describe the dress she had worked so hard on, Mathilde insisted that she would not reveal any details until he saw it on their wedding day at the end of the summer.

Louis would never get that chance.

On July 31, the townsfolk's cries shattered the laziness of the hot summer day. "The English are at the foot of the falls," they said in panic. "They come to take Quebec out of France's hands!"

With great courage and bravery, Louis volunteered to join the French soldiers to defend his land. Mathilde begged him to remain by her side, but a priest convinced her to take supplies and hide in the forest with the other women and children. With a heavy heart, Louis hugged his fiancée and promised he'd return to her.

Mathilde languished in the woods. Listening to the chaotic sounds of battle without being able to see what was happening frayed her nerves and drove her mad with worry. Louis was strong but he wasn't a trained soldier. She feared the worst.

The Battle of Montmorency lasted for days but ended in victory for the French. Relief began to pour through the camp in the woods as the surviving soldiers and towns- men returned to their loved ones. Mathilde waited and waited, begging for news from the men.

"Louis Tessier!" she called in vain. "Has anyone seen him?"

No one answered.

Unable to sit and wait any longer, she ran out of the woods and along the river without caution. She passed soldiers living, dying and dead. Still she called for Louis. Still she was met with stony silence.

Maybe he returned home, she thought and raced to their village, only to find that the English had set it on fire. In the first small shred of good fortune to smile on her since Louis had left for battle, their home stood untouched. She raced inside and searched in the dark for her love but found no trace of him. Mathilde grabbed her wedding dress, hugged it to her chest and ran back outside. The dress glowed faintly in the moonlight.

British attack near Beauport and Mount Morency Falls

Not knowing where to search next, Mathilde finally heard voices calling her name.

Hoping for a miracle, she approached the men who had beckoned her but felt her spirits drop. Their grim faces were drawn tight as a snare drum as they parted to let her pass. And there, lying face down in the dirt on the shore, was a man she instantly recognized.

Mathilde was too late. Louis was dead.

Consumed by grief, Mathilde climbed the hill and stood at the top of the falls. Acting as if in a trance, she slipped into her wedding dress, the dress she would never get to reveal to her groom. She spread her arms out to her sides, looked down upon Île d'Orléans as she had done what felt like a lifetime ago with Louis, and leapt off the edge.

Her body was never recovered.

That hasn't stopped her from returning at night with the moon, scouring the shores for her one true love. Perhaps, had Louis's spirit remained by her side, Mathilde would have found peace. Instead, her anguished moans, carried on the wind, terrorize locals and tourists alike. The inhabitants of Île d'Orléans know to remain in the safety of their homes when the Woman in White is afoot. It's said that anyone who touches her ill-fated wedding dress will die a sudden and horrible death a few days later.

Other than Mathilde, that dress was meant to be touched by one person and one person only.

THE MAN IN THE MIRROR

White Rock, British Columbia

One cold winter night, Jeremy Ellis was closing the Washington Avenue Grill. It was 1:30 a.m. Ellis was alone. The moonlight reflected brightly off freshly fallen snow outside. The neighbourhood was quiet and calm.

Unexpected and unannounced, an odd-looking man barged into the restaurant and startled Ellis, who was nearly ready to head home. "I'm a ghost hunter," the stranger said and urgently asked to investigate the restaurant right there and then. It was as if he had no idea how late the hour was, nor how much of a burden his request would be. Showing the self-proclaimed ghost hunter to the door, Ellis politely denied the request and hoped the man would be understanding. Luckily, he left without further incident.

No sooner had the door closed when the lights began to flicker on their own. Then Ellis happened to look at one of the restaurant's mirrors. There, standing behind him, he saw the reflection of a shadowy figure — an old man. When he spun around no one was there. He raced downstairs and made sure all the doors were locked — they were — and then searched the restaurant to see if he was well and truly alone. There was no sign of either the ghost hunter or the shadowy man he'd seen in the mirror.

The Washington Avenue Grill is located in a yellow building that overlooks Semiahmoo Bay. Their menu features upscale Pacific Northwest cuisine while their dessert menu lists something you might not expect to find in your typical restaurant: a true ghost story.

Before the restaurant opened in 1997, the building served many different purposes. It was built in 1913 by the Campbell River Lumber Company and operated as a lumber mill that employed up to four hundred workers during World War I. After the mill closed, the building became a Presbyterian church, a schoolhouse and a boarding house for migrant railway workers. In 1934 it became the house of Edward Sharpe, a caretaker responsible for the building and the property surrounding it. Sharpe's tragic story is the one that graces the dessert menu.

By all accounts Sharpe was a peculiar man and a bit of a loner. He shunned all human contact and never ventured into town. His days were spent puttering around the old building and tending to the grounds. Sharpe was such a solitary creature that no one could recall ever hearing him speak, but there came one night when his painful screams were impossible to miss.

On a cold November night in 1943, a wicked storm raged through White Rock, forcing the locals into the safety of their homes where they locked their doors and lit fires for warmth. Although the storm was deafening and everyone was inside on that fateful night, most of the townsfolk thought they could hear anguished wails echo through the surrounding hills.

Life returned to normal after the storm. Or at least it seemed to at first. But then people began to realize old man Sharpe hadn't been seen tending to the property for a few days. Daily tasks had been left undone. A search of the grounds found that he had disappeared without a trace, leaving his belongings behind.

The locals began to speculate as to what happened to Sharpe. Some claimed he'd been hit by a train the night of the storm. Others said he had decided to go for a late night polar bear swim and drowned. A few believed the years of solitude had gotten the better of him and he finally snapped, taking his own life. Regardless of which story they believed, everyone agreed the wails they had heard that night were the final sounds Sharpe would utter in this world.

But they didn't know he would come back.

These days, his spirit is far from pleasant, which makes perfect sense. Sharpe was a man who hated company, and now his private residence is filled with restaurant goers — intruders — day in and day out. He expresses his displeasure by turning the lights on and off, moving objects about the restaurant and even damaging the property. One time the handle suddenly broke off a coffee pot and sailed across the room. Another time half the restaurant's selection of wine bottles flew from the wall and shattered on the floor. Objects have been known to explode without warning. And restaurant staff love to recall the time two burly, tattoo-covered busboys ran from the back of the kitchen in a dead panic. They had seen a bin lift itself in the air and then hurtle across the room. The incident had left them as pale as a couple of ghosts.

It also seems Sharpe has found his voice in the after-life. People hear him moaning and yelling in the walls and ceilings of the restaurant. Others have felt him rush past and push them from behind. Like the night Ellis was startled by the appearance of the old man's reflec-tion, Sharpe's favourite scare tactic is to appear suddenly in mirrors. Owner Brent Gray recalls the time a woman walked quickly out of the bathroom, reported that she had seen a spirit in the mirror and said she'd never return to the restaurant.

Some of the restaurant's patrons have reported see-ing other ghosts float across the street in front of the Washington Avenue Grill and enter the dining room late at night. The trouble-making spirits rattle tables, whistle in the basement and play with diners' hair. Oddly, they always take care to leave the restaurant before it gets too late. They know something, it would seem, that we don't.

The ghost of Edward Sharpe demands to be left alone. Although the living have yet to fully comply, the dead are careful to keep a safe distance from the caretaker after nightfall.

ONCE UPON A DEATH

Ottawa, Ontario

The Fairmont Chateau Laurier is a hotel that resembles a fairy-tale castle. Built of limestone with turrets that reach to the sky, it's situated beside the Parliament Buildings in our nation's capital. It's as much a historic landmark as it is a place of lodging, having welcomed kings and queens, princes and princesses, movie stars and famous athletes.

But beneath the hotel's happily-ever-after appearance lies something decidedly less radiant. Something sinister. Whispers and rumours travel the city's streets, warning locals and tourists that a night spent in the Chateau Laurier is a night spent sleeping with the dead.

One young couple who recently stayed for a few days hadn't heard the ghost stories. After checking in and marvelling at the elegant beauty of their guestroom, they were unprepared for what was to happen next. By the time they checked out, however, they left convinced beyond a shadow of a doubt that the hotel was haunted.

The room, it would seem, was already occupied. And whatever was lurking there didn't seem to appreciate the living company.

The couple got settled in their room. Then the man had some errands to tend to, so the woman stayed behind, alone. She tried to relax but she was filled with an uneasy feeling. Something was wrong. As she tried to figure out what was giving her the creeps, something brushed against her arm. She jumped in fright and scanned her surroundings, but her husband hadn't returned — she was still by herself. Then it happened again — something unseen ran its fingers along her skin. Powerless and petrified, the woman could do nothing but pretend her imagination was playing a trick on her. For the next hour, something unseen continued to brush up against her arm.

Perhaps, like a horror movie cliché, the presence was dwelling in the shadows of her room's closet. Late one evening after a night on the town, she was getting ready for bed when something happened that took her breath away. She was removing her makeup in front of a large mirror. Something caught her attention. In the mirror's reflection, over her shoulder and behind her back, the closet door slowly opened with a creak that cut through the quiet of the night.

The next morning the woman took a nice warm shower and tried to forget all about what had happened. As the water washed away the aches and pains of a sleepless night spent tossing and turning, a hand pressed up against the woman's shoulder blade. She spun around with a gasp. No one was there.

Fairmont Chateau Laurier

The angry spirit that refuses to check out of the Chateau Laurier belongs to Charles Melville Hays, a railway president from turn-of-the-century Canada. Hays oversaw the construction of many grand hotels at major train stops, including the Chateau Laurier. The hotel was named after Canada's seventh prime minister despite the fact that one of Laurier's ministers once called Hays cruel and tyrannical.

Cruel and tyrannical he might have been, but Hays was also an ambitious and exacting project manager. He insisted on approving nearly every minute detail of the hotel's construction, even travelling to Europe to handpick the final furnishings before the grand opening. But as fate would have it, these furnishings, and Hays himself, would never complete the journey home to Ottawa. They sank to the floor of the Atlantic, not far from Newfoundland, where they still remain today. Hays had boarded the RMS

Titanic, the well-known passenger liner that struck an iceberg and sank on April 15, 1912, during its maiden voyage. The Chateau Laurier was due to open on April 26 but the opening was postponed to June. What was meant to be a time of celebration was a sombre affair.

The need to see his hotel in its completed state was too great for death to get in his way, and Hays has been spotted in various parts of the Chateau Laurier. He's most active on the eighth floor, where an executive suite is named in his honour. A shadowy figure that fits his description has been spotted floating through the hallways, and hotel staff regularly hear rattling sounds in empty wings. A man who worked thirty years cleaning guestrooms at the Chateau Laurier experienced many creepy events, but what unnerved him more than anything was the fact that he often needed to clean rooms twice. Time and again he'd finish one room and step outside for the briefest flicker of time, only to return to find the room had been completely messed up again and the furniture rearranged.

The staff know that the hotel is haunted and can prepare themselves for the inevitability that they will, sooner or later, be accosted by a ghost. But many guests who check in for a night or two, like the woman who felt something touch her arm, arrive completely unprepared for the fright of a lifetime. Take, for example, another guest who fled her room for the safety of the lobby because all of her personal belongings had flown through the air on their own. Or the man who didn't believe in ghosts before checking into the hotel on a business trip one late October. Upon his arrival he was overwhelmed by an eerie feeling, as if something was warning him to turn around and leave. Once he was in his room, a new but equally frightening feeling took root deep in his soul: he became very depressed and felt like he was completely alone in the building despite the fact that most of the 429 guest rooms were occupied. The businessman left to clear his head, then returned later that evening and went straight to sleep. But it wasn't long before his sleep was interrupted. In the middle of the night he woke with a start when someone sat down on the bed beside him. He rubbed his eyes. There was no one there, but in the spot where he had felt the person sit down he sensed an energy that slowly drained down into his mattress. How much sleep do you think he got after that? Needless to say, the skeptic had turned into a believer. He returned to Ottawa many times for business but was far too scared to return to the Chateau Laurier.

If you're still not convinced that the hotel is haunted, heed the tale of a trusted journalist who had a bone-chilling night in one of the famed suites. In the 1980s, Patrick Watson, CEO of the Canadian Broadcasting Corporation at the time, was sound asleep when he heard a crack as loud as a gunshot. He sat bolt upright and saw, on a table in the living room, a heavy glass ashtray. Somehow, it had cracked clean in half. The incident left Watson with an uneasy feeling, a sensation that dissipated in the morning but returned the next night when he was awoken by another loud sound, this time from the bathroom. Something had picked up his toiletries kit — which he clearly remembered securing on the counter behind the taps — and thrown it across the room, scattering the contents across the floor. Like the broken ashtray, there was simply no way to explain the phenomenon, and Watson admitted to being left quite shaken from his stay in the Chateau Laurier.

Spend a night in this fairy-tale hotel and you might not live so happily ever after, after all.

THE HAUNTED CASTLE IN THE WOODS

Ignace, Ontario

The wilderness of Northern Ontario is a magical place, full of mystery and beauty. The locals are fond of saying there's more water than land. Most of the best camping sites near Ignace are only accessible by boat or plane in the summer and snowmobiles in the winter. It's a popular area for outdoorsy people in search of unspoiled nature. At night, the stars shine brilliantly in the sky and the only sounds are the wind, the wildlife and, along the shores of White Otter Lake, the unsettling wanderings of a hermit ghost.

In the early 1990s, a man and his family canoed into White Otter Lake, unaware of what lay before them. Part of Turtle River Provincial Park, the lake is undeveloped and pristine. There are no lived-in homes or cottages. Like many who have explored the lake before them, the family was shocked when they turned a bend and saw, on the opposite shoreline, a huge, rustic mansion standing out among the trees. What was it doing there? Did anyone live in such a remote location, and if so, who? The allure of the building pulled them toward it as firmly as a giant pair of claws.

The three-storey log cabin was built entirely from huge red pine logs that appeared to weigh a ton. It had a four-storey lookout tower set with windows in each of the four walls. The roof, although faded, was red. The house didn't appear to be occupied and its interior was completely empty. The walls were covered with graffiti. The family had unwittingly stumbled upon White Otter Castle.

Outside, a short distance from the front door, was a wooden grave marker. It had a cross-shaped hole carved straight through its centre. Surrounding the grave were four short wooden fence-boards. The weed-choked ground at the foot of the grave marker was covered by a pile of rocks. One rock was larger than the others and had a name written on it: Jimmy McOuat.

Although it was a little creepy, the man and his wife decided to pitch their tent and spend the night before moving on in the morning. They sat around a fire, the soothing crackle of the burning wood providing a soft soundtrack to their conversation. The silver moon filled the sky and glistened on the lake's surface. Something rustled in the woods — an animal, most likely, and a big one by the sound of it.

The kids decided to call it a night and slipped into their tent. Their mother wasn't long after them. The father remained by the fire alone for a short spell before joining his family. He doused the fire with a good amount of water and then covered the entire firepit in sand. Once the fire

White Otter Castle

was completely out and not even a single wisp of smoke remained, he joined his family and fell asleep.

A few hours later he was awoken by an odd sound: a crackling fire. Flickering orange light filtered through the canvas siding of the tent. Wondering how the fire could have possibly started again on its own, the man unzipped the door flap and poked his head out. He stayed in the tent when he saw that the fire hadn't set itself again — it had been started by a stranger. A ghost.

The spectre sat in the same spot the father had earlier, facing the fire with his back to the tent. He was in his sixties, had a small build, wore a floppy hat and poked the fire with a long stick. The ghost looked over his shoulder, and for a moment the two men — one living, one dead — locked eyes. The ghost silently beckoned for the man to leave the tent and join him, but the father shook his head and hastily zipped the door again (little good that would do to protect his family from a ghost). He managed to drift back to sleep. When he awoke early in the morning he stepped outside. The ghost was gone, so the man investigated the firepit as the sun rose orange and gold. He had to shake his head again — the pit was exactly as he had left it, covered with sand, before turning in the previous night. There was no sign of freshly charred wood. It was as if the reignited fire had been, like the stranger who tended it, a ghost. All these years later, he still gets chills when he tells the story of the spirit who joined his sleeping family on their camping trip.

The ghost the man saw was Jimmy McOuat, the eccentric hermit who is buried beside White Otter Castle. Amazingly, Jimmy built the mansion in 1915, by himself, at the age of fifty-nine.

Jimmy was the son of Scottish immigrants and the

youngest of six sons. His family moved to Canada in the mid-1800s and settled in the Ottawa Valley, but Jimmy set out on his own when he was thirty-one. He settled in Emo, Ontario, and built a homestead on a half section of prime land, which grew to include two farms owned by the hard-working young man. Despite efforts to find a bride, Jimmy never married and spent the rest of his life alone.

When the gold rush took the country by storm in 1899, Jimmy sold his farms, his home and his land and set out once again, this time to stake his claim. A year later, he had lost everything.

Without a penny to his name but refusing to give up, Jimmy ventured even deeper into the wild and found the remote White Otter Lake, more than 30 kilometres away from the nearest town, in 1903. He picked a secluded location on the north shore and, despite not owning the land, built a small, modest shack. He survived by eating the meat of wild animals he trapped and vegetables he grew in a small garden.

Time passed slowly and Jimmy was content to live the life of a forest hermit, but as he grew older he was troubled by a childhood memory. When he was a young boy he had a good friend who was a bit of a prankster. One day, this friend threw an ear of corn and hit a cranky, ill-tempered neighbour of theirs. The man spun on his heel and accused Jimmy of throwing the corn. With flushed cheeks and fire in his eyes, the man cursed young Jimmy.

"Jimmy McOuat," he spat. "Ye'll never do any good! Ye'll die in a shack!"

Years later on the shores of White Otter Lake, this scene played over and over in Jimmy's mind like an old movie that never stopped. He sat alone in his shack and wondered if the grumpy old man's curse would come true.

It certainly seemed as if it would, unless Jimmy did something. And so, despite his age and slight build, Jimmy set about building himself a castle in the woods. Being a Canadian castle, it was fittingly made of logs. He felled the trees, dragged them across his property with a homemade winch and somehow lifted each one into place (the tower walls, for example, are forty-three logs tall and each log weighs well over 350 kilograms). He did all this without the aid of machinery, horses or other workers.

He added one final, morbid addition to the property: his own grave. He was afraid that, after his death, he'd be buried in a cemetery far from his castle, and the curse would follow him into the afterlife.

By the time he had finished White Otter Castle, Jimmy had the last laugh. "Ye couldn't call it a shack, could ye?" he said with pride. "No, ye couldn't call it a shack. An' I built it all myself."

But it's best not to tempt fate, for fate can be cruel. In 1918, shortly after he finished building his castle in the woods, Jimmy mysteriously disappeared. His body was discovered in the lake a year later by a fire ranger. Evidence suggested he had become entangled in his own fishing nets and drowned. Grotesquely, his head and arms had become detached from his body and were never recovered. But what remained of Jimmy was buried in the grave of his own making, as per his wishes.

Perhaps he couldn't bring himself to leave his beloved log mansion after he died, or perhaps he didn't manage to break the curse and is condemned to remain there forever. Whatever the case, the ghost of Jimmy McOuat has been spotted by many campers and outdoors enthusiasts spending a night in or near his home. The provincial government has erected a plaque telling his story, and volunteers work tirelessly to keep White Otter Castle in good condition. They've put one of the only photos of Jimmy, wearing his floppy hat, on an interior wall in the hopes it will give his spirit a little rest, but it doesn't seem to be working.

In life, Jimmy McOuat wished to live on his own. It's not hard to believe that, in death, he might still prefer to roam the Earth in solitude. Some things that hide deep in the woods are better left alone.

THE BLUE NUN

Antigonish, Nova Scotia

Before the residence closed in 2013, first-year students moving into Mount Saint Bernard College at St. Francis Xavier University were issued a dire warning.

"Make sure your chair is tucked tightly under your desk before you go to sleep," upper-year students told new arrivals in all seriousness. "Or else the Blue Nun will take a seat . . . and watch you through the night."

The unexplained phenomena were so prevalent and widespread that midnight visits from the Blue Nun became a rite of passage for St. Francis Xavier (StFX for short) students living on campus. After studying late at night, students would wake to see their chair — which they were certain they had left in its usual place at their desk — dragged across the room to face their bed. Others claimed they had been awoken by the faint blue glow of the ghost nun and saw her sitting, watching. As scary as that sounds, one particular student was targeted by the ghost over a much longer period that culminated in an absolutely petrifying event.

One day after class, the young man returned to his dorm room. He unlocked the door, took a step inside and was instantly confronted by an upsetting sight. All of his books and other belongings — clothes, food, toiletries — had been strewn across the room. The likely assumption was that a fellow schoolmate was engaging in a juvenile prank. But no one else had a key to the room. Nobody owned up to the incident. Then a few days later, it happened again. And again a few days after that. As doubt and fear consumed him, the only solace the student could find in the troubling disturbance was that it only happened when he wasn't in the room.

That would soon change.

After putting everything he owned back in its place for the umpteenth time, the boy fell into a deep slumber. His sleep didn't last long, interrupted by a loud crash as a pile of textbooks, far too heavy to be moved by a draft, toppled off his desk to the floor. Like the phenomenon that was occurring while he was away from his room, this midnight mess became a regular happening in the weeks ahead.

With the lack of sleep came a troubling question. Who was responsible for this targeted attack? The boy soon had his answer, although in no way, shape or form was it a comforting one.

He was awoken in the middle of the night one final time, but not by the crash of falling books. Instead, hovering directly above his bed, was a dark, shadowy being. It stared down at him intently with red, glowing eyes. He opened his mouth but found he was unable to scream. The red-eyed shadow pointed down at him menacingly with a long, bony finger and then dissipated into the air like a cloud of smoke, never to be seen again.

There's a story, widely circulated around the StFX campus, to shed some light on the Blue Nun's existence. Mount Saint Bernard College was originally a college for Catholic women and became North America's first to initiate post-secondary degree programs for women in 1897. Classes were taught by the nuns of the Congrégation de Notre Dame, but a gradual shift occurred and classes were taught by the university. The Mount, as it's commonly known, became a co-ed residence for first- and second-year StFX students.

Mount Saint Bernard College

While the Mount was in the hands of the Congrégation de Notre Dame, it's believed that a nun fell in love with a priest. She became riddled with guilt and fell into a deep depression from which she would never resurface. She walked up to the Mount's fourth floor, stepped onto a balcony and, without a moment of hesitation, flung herself over the railing. She died shortly after her body hit the ground below. The priest, distraught with his own guilt following the nun's suicide, hanged himself in one of the Mount's stairwells. Some people believe in a much darker version of the story, claiming that the priest invited the nun to the fourth floor balcony and pushed her over the edge before taking his own life.

Although the priest is also believed to haunt the Mount, watching people walk up and down the stairwell where he committed suicide (one former student even claims to have accidentally caught the priest in a photograph), it's the Blue Nun's spectre that is most often seen and feared. In fact, her actions and behaviour classify her as a poltergeist, a mischievous ghost known for creating loud noises and throwing physical objects in order to terrorize the living. She makes the lights in dorm rooms flicker on and off without moving the switch, turns on the bathroom faucets to full and continues to throw students' belongings around their rooms. She wakes people by slamming doors and turning computers on, even one that wasn't plugged into the wall outlet.

Although most post-secondary students often sacrifice sleep for all-night study sessions, students at StFX are far more tired than most . . . before they've cracked open a single book.

QUEEN OF THE DEAD

St. John's, Newfoundland and Labrador

During the first half of the nineteenth century, St. John's was a rough and tumble outpost and the site of countless bloody deaths. Unwanted and unclaimed bodies piled up quickly, people who had no one to see them to the grave: passengers who had died aboard ships making the long and arduous transatlantic journey from Europe to North America, executed felons who had dropped from the gallows and inmates of the insane asylum who had breathed their last breath.

There were no morgues in the city in the 1840s, so town officials paid a standing salary to one woman, Nancy Coyle, to prepare the not-so-dearly departed for burial. She washed, dressed and prepared bodies for their final rest, right in her own home where she ate and slept.

By all accounts Nancy was exceptionally skilled at her job . . . so skilled, in fact, that she had the power to bring people back from the dead.

One day Nancy was nailing a coffin shut when the deceased Dutch sailor who was about to be buried six feet under suddenly revived with a start. Nancy did the only thing she could think to do: she gave him a drink of rum, followed by another, and the man was himself again. He thanked her for her services, informed her he'd no longer require the casket and promptly left her home.

Another time, late in the evening after a hard day's work, Nancy covered a fresh corpse in her parlour under a white sheet. The dead man was John Murphy, a man who'd spent many years in an insane asylum and was due to be buried the following morning. Nancy left the parlour and went to bed.

She couldn't sleep. There was an odd noise coming from her parlour. She was convinced she was mistaken. Nancy lived alone and there was no one else in the house. Just her . . . and the bodies.

But the noise didn't go away. It was low and disturbing. It slowly grew louder. It sounded like a moan, perhaps that of an animal. Surely that's all it was: an animal, possibly wounded, that had somehow gotten into her house. She warily got out of bed, lit a candle, hugged her nightdress around her torso and tiptoed through the creaky old home to the parlour.

The moaning turned to groaning and was even louder now. She gripped the door handle with shaking fingers and hesitated a moment before finding the fortitude to open it. It swung open with a shrill creak.

With a glance around the room, Nancy quickly realized there was no animal inside — just John, his body beneath the sheet where she had left it.

Unhhh . . .

There was the groan again. Had it come from under the table that held John's covered body? No, there was nothing underneath.

She crossed the room. Shadows danced on the walls around her, animated by the flickering candlelight she held before her. She placed the candle down and pinched the white sheet between her forefinger and thumb. Then, summoning all her courage, Nancy pulled the sheet away from his face.

The corpse's eyes flew open. They stared up at Nancy, deep into her own wide eyes. She gasped and jumped back. John slipped off the table and fled from her house. For days afterward his reanimated body was seen shambling through the streets and dark alleys in St John's, muttering to himself and yelling at passersby.

The townsfolk were already leery of Nancy Coyle, the lady who spent her days working with bodies and her nights sleeping under the same roof as the dead. But when word began to spread that she had supernatural powers that could bring the dead back to life, she was practically ostracized. She continued her life's work, but when she died in her parlour years later — friendless and alone — there was no one willing to do for her what she had done for the other outcasts who had died in the city. There is no marked grave for Nancy Coyle. No one knows what happened to her body.

People know all too well, on the other hand, what happened to her soul.

Newfoundlanders have seen Nancy's ghost, wearing a long red cloak, wandering through the city's cemeteries alone in the dark. She keeps her head down and answers to no one, a loner in the night. When approached she disappears. Others have seen her leading a ghostly horse-drawn hearse along streets near cemeteries, startling people who had gone to pay their respects.

One such unfortunate person was Bradley Smith, who was standing silently before his aunt's headstone as the moon rose in the sky. It was the sort of night when shadows seem to skitter along the ground and every root and rock poking through the dirt looks like skeletal hands clawing their way out of the earth. Bradley was about to leave when he saw Nancy walking toward him. She was wearing her old-fashioned red cloak. Her face, framed by the hood, was sad and pale. Unaware that she was as dead as the bodies that were buried all around him, Bradley asked Nancy if she was okay. She didn't answer. Thinking she hadn't heard him, he called again and approached. As she passed by, she suddenly vanished in the moonlight.

Bradley said it was the strangest thing he had ever seen and left him feeling terribly frightened. Years after the incident, he still isn't able to go back to that cemetery alone, not even during the day.

It's sad to think Nancy Coyle, the Queen of the Dead, spent her life preparing bodies for burial and no one was willing to do so for her in return. And if she truly could bring back the dead, it's unfortunate she wasn't able to do so for herself. Then again, since she haunts cemeteries and watches over row upon row of decomposing bodies, you could say she *has* cheated death. Despite this, she doesn't seem to be able to rest in peace.

THE NAHKAH

Trout Lake, Northwest Territories

In a small northern community only reachable by bush plane, very few people can hear you scream.

In the late 1960s and early 1970s, however, the fifty-one residents of Trout Lake, located in the Northwest Territories near the British Columbia border, did a lot of screaming. There was a being lurking in the woods, a phantom that tormented the locals over a five-year period. They called him the Nahkah, or "bushman." He was a tall, intimidating figure who stirred up a great deal of panic and fear by hiding in the cover of the surrounding woods, spying on residents. A small ghost dog was sometimes seen by his side. He also had one of the oddest habits imaginable for a ghost.

He liked to play dead.

A young girl and her brother were outside chopping wood one day, pitching in to help their family. As they walked along a wooded path with armfuls of freshly hewn logs, they encountered the Nahkah. He was laying facedown in the dirt like a dead man. They soon discovered he was a dead man, but not in the way they had initially thought. As quick as a flash the Nahkah flew to his feet and floated toward the startled children with his arms outstretched and anger in his eyes. A dog materialized at his feet, yipping hollowly. The siblings dropped the wood and ran away as fast as they could. Luckily, they escaped before he could catch them.

Today Trout Lake is still a small, isolated community. Fewer than one hundred people call the village home, the majority of whom belong to the Dehcho First Nations. Mail is delivered weekly by plane and residents can order books and movies through the Northwest Territories Public Library Services' Borrow by Mail Program. People can reach Trout Lake in the winter by road, but the only way in or out the rest of the year is by plane. The Royal Canadian Mounted Police were called in to investigate the strange case of the Nahkah after they received complaints from local fishermen and families reporting that the spectral bush man had stolen fish from their nets and caribou and moose meat from their drying racks. Unsurprisingly, the authorities found no trace of the apparition and soon left. But the Nahkah continued to haunt the area.

He usually appeared at dusk as the sun was setting behind the trees across the lake. While enjoying dinner, families would glimpse a man's face peering in through the windows of their cabins moments before disappearing. Parents and children would rush outside to discover the

Nahkah had vanished, leaving behind a trail of ghostly footprints that led into the woods.

The residents concluded the apparition must dwell in the surrounding open spruce forest, gliding above the moss- and berry-carpeted floor with his dog. Some argued that the Nahkah might be a living man, but that theory was quickly rejected. No man could survive on his own without a dwelling, with winter lows of -50°C and ice that lasts on the lake well into June. Trout Lake is nearly 1,000 kilometres northwest of Edmonton, separated from Yellowknife by Great Slave Lake and virtually impossible to reach from the nearest community on foot, so the Nahkah couldn't be travelling to and from the community. The only explanation was that the bushman was actually a bush *ghost*.

Still, there were skeptics, including Chief Joseph Jumbo, who thought the Nahkah didn't exist at all. But then, one day, he had his own encounter with the Nahkah that completely changed his opinion of the mysterious man in the woods. He had seen much in his seventy-seven years and, after confronting the Nahkah himself, spared little time for anyone who believed the shadowy intruder was a product of anyone's imagination.

While setting his fishing nets in the mouth of one of Trout Lake's creeks, Jumbo caught a glimpse of a man following him in the bushes along the bank. It was the Nahkah, taunting the chief by whistling at him.

Not one to be easily intimidated or frightened, Jumbo stood and faced the Nahkah directly. "I'm chief here," he proclaimed. "If you come out into the open we'll be happy to give you anything you might need. Food, clothing or moccasins."

Despite the kindness of the chief's offer, the Nahkah

refused to answer or show himself, as if he had disappeared once again. Jumbo would later admit to a reporter that he began to get very scared at that moment. He would've been happy to aid the Nahkah or leave him alone, so long as he knew what he wanted and who — or what — he was. But the shadowy man's silence worried Jumbo. He feared the Nahkah might do something to Trout Lake's children, maybe even steal one away into the woods. He had, after all, come after the young siblings chopping wood.

Fortunately, as time passed the Nahkah was rarely seen again. After five years, he disappeared altogether. What didn't disappear so quickly was the fear the ghostly bushman had instilled in the residents of Trout Lake. That, like ice on a northern lake, took a lot longer to fully melt away.

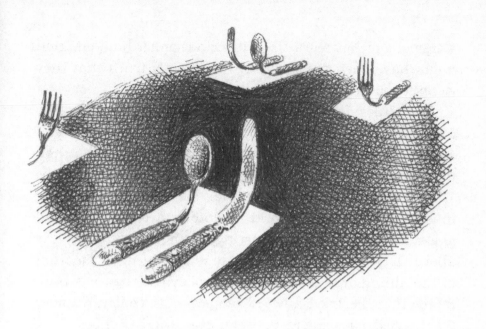

THE GHOST CONDUCTOR

Vancouver, British Columbia

Darkness had settled like a heavy cloak upon Gastown, Vancouver's oldest neighbourhood. It was the middle of the night and The Old Spaghetti Factory was nearly empty. The final customers and most of the restaurant's employees had gone home. Only two people remained, but they weren't alone.

Kris Newson, who was a manager at the time, sat at the bar with another manager. They passed the time with sleepy conversation as they waited for their rides to pick them up. Suddenly, a large shadow in the shape of a man leapt onto the bar between them, causing every hair on Newson's body to stand on end. After the shadow disappeared, Newson asked the other manager if he had seen the apparition. He had, confirming that the ghost wasn't a figment of Newson's tired imagination. A hallucination might have been preferable to the ghastly truth that they were in the presence of the dead.

The Pulos family brought The Old Spaghetti Factory franchise from the United States to Canada in 1970 and opened the Gastown location in an old building that had previously been a train station, general store and factory. The restaurant is filled with antique artifacts and furnishings from around the world, including a piece of stained glass from the Queen's Carriage. But there's one piece above all else that is impossible to miss. Sitting in the front of the dining area is an original trolley car that was built by the B.C. Electric Railway Company. The trolley, Number 53, carried passengers between Main and Cambie every day from 1904 to 1950. When it was taken out of service it was moved to the Pacific National Exhibition grounds where it sat unused for twenty years before being loaned to the restaurant.

Once installed inside The Old Spaghetti Factory the trolley was converted to include tables and chairs. But the Pulos didn't know what they were bringing into their restaurant or else they might have had second thoughts. The trolley came with a conductor — a man who had died in the early 1900s and refused to leave No. 53 despite the trolley's new location and purpose.

It's believed that the conductor died in a train accident near Waterfront Station, just down the street from the restaurant. His ghost is regularly seen inside the decommissioned trolley late at night, often sitting at the same table. People on the trolley have walked through cold spots and witnessed the table settings moving on their own.

The trolley is the most photographed area of The Old Spaghetti Factory. And upon reviewing their photographs, some people have discovered the conductor has been captured by their camera. One such photo hangs on the restaurant's walls. It shows a misty apparition, which many believe to be the conductor himself, hovering on the trolley's steps.

Although he's the most well-known of the restaurant's spirits, the conductor isn't the only one. At least three other spirits dwell within, and they aren't all as tame.

A little girl sits at a table by the front window. She holds a single balloon by a string and waits for people to stop and chat with her. A friend of the general manager once saw her and, unaware that the girl didn't have a pulse, struck up a lively conversation. The ghost girl said she was waiting for her mother. Thinking he should inform the manager, he turned and called to the bar. When he looked back at the table, the little girl had disappeared into thin air.

A little boy with a naughty streak haunts the back of the restaurant. He stands out from the regular clientele

Photo of the trolley car that hangs in The Old Spaghetti Factory

thanks to the period clothing he wears — a brown vest over a beige long-sleeved shirt with a miner's cap perched atop his disheveled hair. He likes to run around the restaurant, particularly after it has closed for the night, calling out employees' names and hiding in dark corners or under tables. One night a staff member set the cutlery on each of the back tables so it would be ready when the restaurant opened again the next day. As soon as he had finished he looked up from his task and was stunned to discover that all the cutlery had been bent up toward the ceiling. Positive his eyes must be playing tricks on him, he called his co-workers who confirmed the cutlery truly had been bent. They went to fetch a manager, but when they all returned, the cutlery had been bent back without any earthly explanation.

The boy in old clothing has also been seen trailing waiters through the restaurant. One night, a server confronted the boy and asked where his parents were. The boy demanded that some music be put on so the other ghosts would come out. Shortly after making this odd request he disappeared.

Another waitress chased down what she thought was a young customer through the dining area after the restaurant had closed. She looked deep into his dead eyes and immediately walked to the front of the restaurant, reported the incident to her manager and quit on the spot. She couldn't bear the thought of spending one more night in the company of the dead boy.

The fourth ghost is the most mischievous of the lot and has often been described as "devilish" and "demonic." Appropriately attired from head to toe in red clothing, with flushed cheeks and bright red hair, he's come to be known as "The Little Red Man." He spends his time in the restaurant's bathrooms and scares customers when they're least expecting it. When all is quiet and it appears as if no one else is in the room, The Little Red Man suddenly appears and cackles before quickly exiting the bathroom. Sometimes he dissolves into a swirling black cloud in the stalls, as witnessed by an employee who was closing the restaurant one night. He's never been seen in any other part of the restaurant. Two women once took his picture in the women's bathroom, presumably to report him to the police, but when they looked at the photo there was only a black cloud where The Little Red Man had stood before them.

To shed some light on the paranormal activity, restaurant staff brought in a psychic at one time. While examining the dining area, the psychic identified the ghost of a boy named Edward, and also discovered what she believed to be a vortex where Edward is often seen playing late at night. The vortex, the psychic explained, is tied to the Earth's electromagnetic fields and might be acting as a portal to other dimensions, which has allowed spirits to enter the restaurant over the years. She also confirmed that many of the heirlooms and antiques in the dining room, including the trolley car, have ghosts attached to them.

More recently, a group of students spent a few harrowing nights in the restaurant. During their first term at the Vancouver Film School, director Michelle Doherty and producer Elise McMullen created a documentary about the paranormal activity in The Old Spaghetti Factory. The two students shared an interest in ghosts, and Michelle used to live beside the restaurant. She always felt a cold, eerie energy when she ate there, so it was the perfect location for their documentary. They gained permission to film in the establishment after open hours from manager Andre Pastor, brought in a well-known medium named Derrick Whiteskycloud, assembled their small crew and got to work.

They filmed for a few nights after all the customers had left. Elise recalls the feeling of unease she experienced while working on the documentary. Although she feels silly about it now, she and Michelle refused to go anywhere alone. They felt as if someone was watching them the entire time they were there.

Late one night Andre and Derrick were walking around the dining area describing what they were feeling and trying to get the spirits to do something while the cameras rolled. Much to everyone's shock, the spirits decided to answer. A series of loud bangs and creaks broke the silence behind them, but there was no one there. The temperature suddenly plummeted and goose bumps prickled across Derrick's skin. Something messed with the students' film equipment and the audio became distorted, a common tendency of active ghosts.

"They're here," Derrick proclaimed in a voice eerily reminiscent of a horror movie.

Not only are "they" there in The Old Spaghetti Factory, they show no sign of leaving anytime soon.

HOTEL HELL

Toronto, Ontario

Long ago, back when the Fairmont Royal York was not only the tallest building in Toronto but in the entire British Commonwealth, a wealthy gentleman and his new bride checked into the hotel on their wedding night. The bride had visions of the dancing they'd enjoy in the ballroom, the delicious meals they'd eat in each of the hotel's restaurants and the sights they'd take in around the city. The groom, however, had a different honeymoon in mind. His intentions were as dark and bloody as the burgundy smoking jacket he wore when they checked in.

That very night, their bellies still full of wedding cake and champagne, the husband murdered his wife where she slept. He then took his own life, leaving behind a gory, horrific scene for a cleaning woman to find the next morning. No one knows why the man committed such an atrocity on what should have been the happiest night of his life, but present-day staff at the Royal York agree that their deaths were too tragic for either spirit to ever check out of the hotel.

A former staffer had heard the stories, but he didn't believe in ghosts. The story of the murderous groom was just that, a story. His co-workers were simply trying to give him a fright.

But then one night he worked a double shift and was allowed to stay in one of the 1,600 guest rooms. By coincidence — or maybe it was fate — the employee was checked into the murder room. He still wasn't fazed. There's no such thing as ghosts.

Right?

Exhausted from the day, the man slipped under the covers and turned out the light. Nothing could have prepared him for what lurked in the shadows, watching over him as he drifted in and out of sleep. Sometime later he woke up and checked the clock. It was 3 a.m. But the clock wasn't the only thing glowing in the darkness. On the other side of the bedroom a strange light floated above the ground. Before he could do anything — scream, hide or flee — he heard a door slowly swing shut in the suite's sitting room. He found the nerve to slip out of bed, or maybe he just needed to get away from the ghostly light, and found that the door had not only swung shut, but the bolt had been turned, locking it tight.

He wasted no time scrambling back into his bed, but comfortable as the mattress and sheets might have been, he didn't sleep the rest of the night.

The Royal York has been described as a "city within a city block." It's no longer the tallest building in Toronto —

Fairmont Royal York Hotel

far from it — and is now surrounded by glass and metal skyscrapers. But in a way, with its bright-red electric sign and Gothic motifs, the hotel appears even more grand and elegant now that it sits hunched amidst modern architecture, a ghostly historical imprint from a different time. Since it opened in 1929, the Royal York has welcomed more than forty million guests — it's only natural that a few have refused to leave. Ever.

Being such a large, twisty, labyrinthine building, there are more than enough hidden nooks and crannies for each of the Royal York's shadows and spirits to hide.

There's the wealthy wife-murderer in the red smoking jacket. He's often seen wandering the eighth floor halls and lurking in the stairwells, while his ghost bride's soul is trapped in the room where she met her grim demise. But these two spirits aren't alone. It's rumoured that a former employee hanged himself in a stairwell that leads to the electrical and maintenance rooms on the floor above the guestrooms. Living employees have seen his body — or, the *top half* of his body — floating through the upper levels. That he no longer has legs is a freaky mystery that haunts those who see him.

The ballroom is another area that is a hotbed for paranormal activity. Employees have seen ghosts gliding and twirling across the dance floor. The crystal chandeliers rattle and shake on their own, threatening to fall from the ceiling. Guests trying to sleep in rooms near the ballroom have called the front desk to complain about the loud music and chatter that had woken them in the middle of the night. The standard answer — that there wasn't a party or function taking place in the ballroom that evening — raises more questions, questions most would rather not have answered. Is it possible that the ghosts of the upper class, who used to attend the hotel's famed dances during the first half of the twentieth century, still gather from time to time to relive their glory days?

Some believe a tragic event that occurred near the hotel might be responsible for some of the ghosts who linger in its halls. In 1949, when the SS *Noronic*, the largest passenger cruise ship on the Great Lakes, caught fire in Toronto harbour, the hotel's lobby was quickly transformed into a field hospital. Sadly, 139 people lost their lives that day.

In the years following this tragedy, guests began reporting an unusual sound: children running through the halls in the middle of the night. These unsettling reports continue today. After a long day working on his latest book, author Christopher Heard, who writes in the hotel, was awoken by small footsteps pounding up and down the hallway outside his room, followed by peals of laughter. He approached his door and looked out the peephole. Oddly, the noises continued — left to right, right to left, directly outside his room — but he couldn't see anyone in the hallway. He opened his door and stepped outside. The playful sounds of running and laughing ceased immediately. No one was there. A doorman later confided that Heard wasn't the first to hear the ghost children who tear up and down the hotel's halls at night, nor would he be the last.

Tragedy, suicide, murder. If you believe the stories shared by the hotel's employees, the Royal York has seen it all. And if buildings had a mind of their own, the old hotel would wish it could *unsee* some of its past. But the souls of those who have died there will never let that happen.

DREAM A LITTLE NIGHTMARE

Lac La Biche, Alberta

It's quite common for people who have had paranormal encounters to report feelings of being watched. For a select unfortunate few, the feelings go much further. Much darker. It's possible to feel that the spirit watching you has entered your body and possessed your soul.

On the last day of her trip to Lac La Biche, a woman in her thirties named Isabelle decided on a whim to visit the Lac La Biche Mission with her children, sister and nieces. They had heard rumours that the mission was haunted by a priest who had died there. Had Isabelle known what would happen to her at the mission that fateful day, she likely wouldn't have gone anywhere near it.

Finding herself walking among the tombstones, Isabelle was drawn to one in particular. She didn't know what about it had attracted her and the name and dates etched in the stone were obscured by a thick layer of dirt. She bent down and wiped the filth away but as soon as she touched the gravestone an ice-cold chill passed into her fingers and shot up her arm, sending her reeling away. It felt like she had been shocked by an electrical current.

The sisters and their kids quickly left the mission and drove back to the hotel. During the drive, Isabelle developed a migraine unlike any she had ever experienced before. She felt as though electricity was crackling in her brain.

When they finally got back to the hotel, Isabelle's sister put the kids to sleep in a separate room. Isabelle crawled into her own bed and tumbled into a fretful sleep. That's when the dreams started.

Isabelle saw herself running in a field. Thanks to dream logic — or perhaps something supernatural — she knew she was a young girl named Emma Ladouceur and that she'd been born in the Lac La Biche Mission. At the far end of the field was a large man, possibly Emma's father, leaning against a barn. The man had a thick moustache and Isabelle (or Emma) could tell he was furious with her.

The dream jumped ahead in time and Isabelle/Emma was lying in bed. An old woman fretted about the room, her worry plainly written on her face. Isabelle's body was painfully cold despite the thick sheets piled atop her chest. She knew then that she was dying.

Isabelle's sister, meanwhile, sat at her sister's side on the hotel bed and watched helplessly as Isabelle began to speak in her sleep.

"I'm dying, Mommy," Isabelle whispered. "I'm going to die."

The sister became more concerned as the dream grew

more intense. Isabelle began to shake uncontrollably, as if dreaming of the dying girl was actually sucking the life out of her grown body.

"You are not my sister," Isabelle's sister shouted at the top of her lungs. "Leave this body now!"

Luckily, the forceful command worked and whatever had entered Isabelle fled from within her. She woke up, relieved to have escaped the terror she had felt while asleep.

Sometime later Isabelle found an old book that contained pictures of all the families that had worked at the mission over the years. Flipping through the pages, she stopped on a random page and couldn't believe her eyes. There, staring back at her from a faded black and white photograph, was the angry man with the moustache. And

House at Lac La Biche with Augustin Ladouceur at left

sitting at his feet was Emma Ladouceur.

Emma was born in 1885 into a large Roman Catholic family that had lived in Lac La Biche for three generations and spoke English, French and Cree. Her father, Augustin, operated a fur trading post with his brothers, a building that burned down in 1970. Not much is known about Emma's life and very few records exist from that time period in Lac La Biche. There is only one photograph of Augustin held in the collections of the Provincial Archives of Alberta, and his face is obscured by a white spot so precisely positioned that it almost seems like it was damaged on purpose. It's hard to pretend that the coincidental location of the photo damage isn't strange, mysterious and even a little creepy. There are no known photos of Emma in the Archives.

Isabelle still has the book with the rare photo of Emma but hasn't been able to bring herself to look at it again. Some memories — and the spirits that haunt them — are better left in the past where they belong.

THE SWAMP HAG

Bell Island, Newfoundland and Labrador

The sun set on Bell Island's western horizon, casting a warm glow across the water and land. But a deep darkness descended swiftly, cold enough to chill your heart. A group of men, weary and exhausted from a full day's work in the mines, hurried to finish their farming chores.

Although work in the iron ore mines in 1943 was plentiful, the pay wasn't great, and some of the men had ten or more children. With so many mouths to feed and so little money to buy food, the men divided the fertile land of Dobbin's Garden and shared the work of growing and tending crops. Potatoes, carrots and cabbage filled their families' supper plates each night thanks to their efforts in the fields.

This night, as the men left one by one to return home

to their families, Nathaniel Hammond pressed on under the cover of darkness. He still had work to do with his potatoes, and he was so focused that he scarcely realized that he was now alone. He worked with his back to the large swamp that was surrounded by spruce trees and tall grass beside Dobbin's Garden.

With sweat coating his forehead and his muscles aching, his nostrils twitched and he detected an odd smell. It was a faint scent of rot, but it grew stronger with every passing second. He stopped working. The odour became so powerful and pungent that Nathaniel's head grew heavy, and he feared he might collapse.

He scanned the land, finally realizing he was the sole worker in the fields. But then he turned to look over his shoulder, and he saw her — a young woman. She had come out of the swamp and was approaching him slowly but deliberately. She wore a tattered and muddy white cloak that covered her head and concealed her face. Beneath the cloak she wore a dress that was covered in holes.

Nathaniel tried to call to her but couldn't even manage to say hello. It was the smell — it filled his mouth, coated his tongue and choked his lungs. It was like eating a rotten egg and washing it down with a mouthful of brackish swamp water. His stomach heaved and his legs suddenly buckled. Nathaniel fell to the ground, confused, disoriented and repulsed.

As he looked to the heavens above, the woman looked down upon him.

Unable to move, short of breath and utterly powerless, Nathaniel lay in the dirt as the woman crouched down at his feet, silently regarding him. The *thing* — that's how Nathaniel began to think of her, for he had decided she was no living woman — slowly crawled on her hands and knees up his body from his feet to his legs to his belly to his chest. Her head hovered mere inches above his. He closed his eyes. Greasy hair tangled with sticks, mud and decaying leaves brushed his nose and chin. Against his better judgment, but overcome with a powerful urge to look at his tormentor, Nathaniel opened his eyes and saw her face. He immediately regretted it.

Her skin was peeling off her skull. Holes covered her nose and cheeks, revealing bone and teeth. Her flesh was rotten and grey. But worst of all were the thing's eyes. Staring down at him with venom were two deep pools of darkness.

When she opened her mouth, her jaw bone cracked. And when she spoke, the nub of her decomposing tongue slithered like a slug in a mud puddle. Her stench was overpowering, so Nathaniel desperately tried to hold his breath.

"You heard me when I cried, pleaded and screamed for help," she hissed, "but you and your kind ignored my pleas. Because of you and your superstitious ways, I died a horrible death in that swamp. Now I have come back to avenge my own death!"

She lowered her face to his, so close that Nathaniel could practically taste the putrid swamp water that oozed from her pores. He gasped for air but couldn't breathe. The world grew darker than he thought possible, and stars danced before his eyes. Nathaniel whispered, "It wasn't me," and then lost consciousness.

Back home, Nathaniel's wife had grown alarmed when he hadn't returned with the other men. She looked for him at their neighbours' houses and discovered he was the last to remain in Dobbin's Garden. When the townsfolk learned Nathaniel was missing, a search party set out with lanterns in hand. They found Nathaniel lying on his back in a drill of potatoes. He wasn't moving, his clothes were covered in muck, and an awful smell wafted off his body. His brother John, who had joined the search party, was the first to kneel down beside Nathaniel. Fearing the worst, John was relieved to discover Nathaniel was still alive. They carried Nathaniel back to his house and called for the local doctor. Dr. Young's first words after arriving and laying eyes on Nathaniel were, "My God, did he fall into an outhouse?"

Nathaniel soon regained consciousness and told the assembled group what had happened to him. The smell, the attack, the woman — the thing. The doctor doubted the story, believing instead that Nathaniel had suffered a seizure and imagined the entire ghastly episode. But that didn't explain why Nathaniel smelled exactly like gassy swamp water. And since that day in 1943, more than two dozen men have been found in Dobbin's Garden, in the same dirty state, with the same story of a woman crawling out of the swamp and attacking them.

Some call her the Hag, others the Ghost of Dobbin's Garden. It's believed that, shortly before 1943, a young woman was picking berries alone when she ventured too far from home, became lost and called for help, but no one came to her rescue. She died in the swamp, alone and scared, cursing the locals who hadn't come to her aid. Fair or not, her vengeful ghost seems intent on terrifying as many Bell Island locals as possible.

Children are warned to stay far away from the swamp. Those who can't avoid Dobbin's Garden are warned to carry a Bible with them at all times. Even the bravest young men and women on the island know better than to be caught alone in Dobbin's Garden after sundown.

A SPINE-CHILLING READ

Barrie, Ontario

A woman stood alone in the cold, quiet night, waiting for a prescription to be filled at a pharmacy in the Wellington Plaza. Most of the shops in the strip mall were closed and empty, including Rivendell Books. Her gaze drifted as the minutes passed. And then she realized the plaza wasn't as deserted as she had thought. She noticed an elderly, grey-haired man in old-fashioned clothing who looked out of place walking back and forth in front of Rivendell Books. It was as if he was upset that the bookstore was closed and was searching for a way in. Then he found it: he approached the door and stepped straight through the glass.

The ghost of the old man is not unknown to the people who work at Rivendell Books. In fact, he might be one of their most loyal customers. He's certainly the most troublesome — frightening patrons as they walk up and down the aisles looking for their next read.

Wendy Cahill, the bookstore owner, has said that multiple odd and disturbing occurrences have taken place in the shop, often late at night when no one else is in the store. Many customers (*living* customers, that is) have seen the old man in the history section, and others have even felt him touch them before disappearing.

One day, while Cahill was in the back, she heard a loud bang in the front of the shop. She rushed through the store, puzzled by the sound and unsure what might have caused it. She found a biography about infamous serial killer Charles Manson lying in the middle of the floor. Someone had thrown it to the ground, but there was no one around. As Cahill stared, somewhat hypnotized, into Manson's cold eyes on the cover of the book, books started flying off the shelves and through the air around her.

Books flying off shelves is usually good for business, but Cahill found no comfort in the ghost's antics. She and her husband often stayed late on Saturday nights to clean and organize after the store had closed. No one else entered the store until the Cahills returned early on Sunday mornings. And yet when they made their way to the back the next day, they were regularly met by a disquieting sight. There, on the floor of the history section, were towers of neatly stacked books reaching high into the air. Most were about World War I and II.

It would be one thing if the ghost was content to remain in the store, but that's not always the case. One unfortunate customer purchased a book to read and enjoy, only to learn he had unwittingly invited a *bibliophantom* into his home.

Derek Ellis, a history buff, wanted to learn more about the Great War, so he browsed Rivendell Books' collection, completely unaware that the store he had entered was haunted. He selected a big book about World War I, paid for it and returned home. He had visited the store by himself, but he did not return home alone. Ellis would soon discover, in the middle of the night, that he had purchased a book that was one of the old ghost's personal favourites, and the spirit had no intention of missing a single night of reading.

A few minutes past midnight, Ellis suddenly woke up and came face to face with the ghost dressed in old-fashioned clothing. He was silently staring at Ellis from the foot of the bed, as if the ghost was angry at Ellis for

Inside Rivendell Books

having purchased the book from the shop. Ellis thought he might still be dreaming, but pinching his face and arms proved that he was awake and the ghost was real. The next day, Ellis did not tell his wife what he had seen for fear of scaring her, and he secretly hoped the midnight appearance would be the last he'd see of the bookstore ghost. It was not.

The next night he awoke after midnight again and smelled the strong aroma of flowers, despite the fact there were none in the room. Then, as he was trying to fall back asleep, a chair beside his bed creaked from the weight of someone sitting down on it. When Ellis rolled over and looked at the chair, it was empty. His cat then leaped onto the bed and stared intently at the empty chair as if sizing up some stranger. It left Ellis feeling very uncomfortable.

The midnight visits continued for the next few nights. On one occasion, Ellis awoke to see a bright red curtain that hadn't been there before, covering his closet door. After a few minutes the curtain suddenly disappeared.

Another night Ellis was woken by the sound of someone flipping through the pages of a book. He looked up and saw the old man standing in front of the closet. The ghost strode toward the bed, returned the World War I book to the nightstand, walked into the closet, waved to Ellis . . . and disappeared.

On the final night Ellis owned the book, he awoke once more to see the old man pacing the room, deep in thought while reading the book. The ghost wandered into the closet and disappeared again, and the book fell to the floor with a bang. Ellis had to retrieve it later.

Ellis began to fear that he was losing his mind, so as a final desperate measure, he took the book and visited a priest. The clergyman did not laugh or brush off Ellis's concerns. Far from it. With deadly urgency, the priest told Ellis he must get rid of the book, and in doing so get rid of the ghost.

Ellis followed the priest's advice and returned the tome of terror to Rivendell Books, but he didn't tell Cahill the real reason — the sinister reason — why he had decided to sell it back to the store. A month later, however, he returned and finally revealed the scary story. Ellis thought Cahill might not believe him, but she grabbed his arm and said, "My God! I do believe you." And then, in an ominous whisper, she added, "You wouldn't believe what's been going on in this shop."

In Rivendell Books, truth is often stranger — and scarier — than fiction.

DEMON HOTEL

Winnipeg, Manitoba

It was early October in 2012 and the first cool wisps of wintry air had begun to chill downtown Winnipeg's back alleys and shadowy corners. Crunchy, rust-coloured leaves swirled across the cracked pavement as the days grew shorter. A photographer and writer who calls himself Urban Explorer had passed by the Demon Hotel, an abandoned apartment building at 44 Hargrave Street, many times. Despite having felt compelled to enter the old building before, he had never built up the courage to do so. It had sat empty for many years, and most of the windows and doors were boarded up.

People who lived in the area had reported seeing pale, elongated faces with red eyes peering out from the few windows that hadn't been covered. It was widely believed that some of these entities were demons that had escaped from the underworld. With nervous laughter, locals often say, "when they're not in Hell, they stay at the Demon Hotel." Other people have spotted ghosts who try to plead for help, but when the spirits open their mouths, not a sound escapes . . . because their tongues have been ripped out from the backs of their throats.

Other locals recount the story of the spray paint that persists in appearing on one of the building's exterior walls. One day the words "DEMON HOTEL" were found painted on a sheet of wood that barred people from entering one of the broken doors. Fearing this ominous proclamation gave the neighbourhood an unsavoury appearance that would be bad for business, the local business association painted over it. Some time later, however, the words reappeared through the fresh coat of paint. More paint was applied to the wood, but once again the words came back. This happened time and again, defying all logic.

Since its construction in 1910, the apartment had seen more than its fair share of tragedy and death. A search of the newspaper archives reveals that in 1926 a resident of the building, Charles Seymour, was struck and killed by a streetcar when crossing Hargrave and Broadway. Seven years later, Mary Sue Burns ran out of the apartment and was killed by a passing Winnipeg Electric Company truck. In 1973, Lorraine Joan Bachinski was stabbed to death in the building.

Despite the bloody history and the all-too-apparent signs that something terribly evil dwelled there, Urban Explorer could no longer resist the call to sneak in to take some pictures of the building's innards.

When no one was looking, he snuck inside as the sun

was beginning to set. He slowly, hesitantly crept along a dark, dingy corridor. Paint was peeling off the walls and the floor was covered in dirt and debris. His nose was immediately assaulted by a revolting smell he described as equal parts decay and . . . something else . . . something not of this world. As he walked deeper into the belly of the building, the temperature dropped rapidly and it became unnaturally cold. He didn't hear any sounds other than his own heavy breathing and the scrape of his shoes, but that was about to change.

The broken and dust-covered stairs creaked loudly as he climbed them. It must have been his imagination, but he could have sworn that he was being watched as he neared the second floor. And then he heard a soft yet distinct sound: rustling in the room ahead. Remarkably, he carried on.

In the centre of the large room, he stopped. The pungent odour intensified. The air grew colder. The rustling became louder. He took a few pictures, and then something creaked above his head on the third floor. *The wind*, he tried to convince himself, *or an animal*. But no, it was no use trying to fool his mind. What he had heard was the unmistakable sound of soft footsteps passing over broken floorboards.

Although he nearly turned and fled, he forced himself to continue upwards. The footsteps above grew louder and more distinct as he quietly climbed to the top. But then he accidentally kicked a broken piece of wood. It tumbled down the stairwell in a series of deafening bangs and crashes before it reached the bottom with a final, deadly crack. He froze. All was silent. Whatever he had heard on the third floor was no longer moving. Had it been his imagination?

Demon Hotel

Suddenly a door slammed on one of the lower levels, the sound echoing up the staircase. Fortunately he had spied a back stairwell — he had no intention of going back down the way he had come. He turned on his flashlight and made his precarious way down. He reached the main floor without incident, but as he peered a little farther down, into the basement, he felt a cold blast of air rush up from below. His flashlight flickered ominously. He should have left then and there, but some mad idea had taken shape in his head. He had come this far and seen nearly all of the Demon Hotel . . . all but the basement. He decided on a whim that he would go a little farther.

He went downstairs.

The nightmare basement was straight out of a horror movie: crumbling stone walls; rusted pipes, wires and hooks dangling from the low ceiling; dark holes in the floor and walls that might have held a hundred unseen terrors; ugly, unmentionable stains splattered in the corners.

After passing through a labyrinthine series of narrow halls and filthy rooms, he was overcome by an oppressive feeling of dread. He needed to get out immediately. He turned to backtrack out of the basement but quickly became disoriented and lost. His flashlight flickered once, twice and then shut off completely. The blackness pressed in on all sides and he couldn't see more than a few feet in any direction.

As Urban Explorer stumbled through the dark praying to find the exit, an evil aura suddenly filled the air, as strong and real as the cold. A spirit he described as "powerful and grotesque" slammed into his body, threw him against one of the crumbling stone walls and pinned his back against it. He fell to the ground and looked around wildly. His eyes landed upon his first stroke of good luck since he had bravely, perhaps foolishly, entered the Demon Hotel at dusk: the staircase was straight ahead. He picked himself up and ran as fast as his legs could carry him, up the stairs, out the door and into the night. He didn't stop running until he was far away. He never looked back.

In a bizarre, macabre twist, the Demon Hotel burned to the ground on April 6, 2015. The fire was blamed on teenage arsonists, but that hasn't stopped the locals from continuing to tell stories and to speculate as to what really happened on Hargrave Street. Many saw the faces and bodies of demons in pictures of the blaze that appeared on social media. Some believe the teens might have snuck into the building on an innocent dare but then became possessed by the spirits that lurked within and set fire to the building against their wills. Others were thankful to see the cursed building reduced to cinders and ash, but dreaded the possibility that the fire had released the ghosts into the city to find new homes. No one wants to think that the maze-like tunnels and rooms of the basement still sit beneath the earth, waiting for some unfortunate soul to discover them.

One thing is certain: the man who goes by the name Urban Explorer will forever wish that he hadn't explored the urban decay of the Demon Hotel.

MUSEUM OF THE PARANORMAL

Niagara-on-the-Lake, Ontario

People come from all over the country — even from around the world — to see her. Day in and day out, she sits on a small, black rocking chair. The rocker, wreathed in shadow, is cornered away in the attic. She waits silently, her skin cracked and her eyes glassy, as people stare, ogle and point at her. Her name is Lizzie, and she's the prime attraction in the Museum of the Paranormal. Lizzie is a doll, but not the type you used to play with when you were younger. Lizzie is haunted.

Stephanie Cumerlato, who owns the museum with her husband, recalls the day Lizzie was donated to them. The previous owners were scared and agitated and needed to rid themselves of Lizzie's haunting presence. Their fear had reached an all-time high and they couldn't keep Lizzie in their house a single day longer. Every time they looked at Lizzie's oddly human face, Lizzie would look back . . . and then wink, as if sharing some sick, private joke.

Stephanie gladly accepted Lizzie and displayed her in the attic. Lizzie settled in and spent her days and nights with, among other attractions, Boris the (real, living) tarantula, a collection of authentic Ouija boards and the museum's collection of rare post-mortem photography. And yes, "post-mortem photography" is exactly what it sounds like: photographs of dead people, often from the Victorian era when families would take pictures of their deceased relatives.

People know they're being watched as soon as they set foot in the creaky attic. Lizzie's eyes follow visitors as if propelled by a dark, evil energy. One evening Stephanie was on the main level when a woman came down from the attic and said in a terrified hush that Lizzie had winked at her. An hour later, another woman entered the museum, climbed the stairs and returned looking as pale as a ghost. Although this second woman didn't know the first woman nor any of the stories surrounding Lizzie, she told Stephanie that Lizzie had winked at her too.

But ghostly goings-on were prevalent in the museum long before Lizzie moved in. The building, dating back to the 1920s, used to be a blacksmith's shop. Tragedy struck the business when the blacksmith's daughter stood too close to the fireplace. A spark flew out from the hearth and ignited the girl's dress in a roaring blaze. Despite attempts to save her life, the girl died. After the blacksmith passed away, people began seeing him and his daughter lingering in the building.

Today lights flicker on and off, faces peer out from the windows after the museum is locked up and the piano

Lizzie in the Museum of the Paranormal

is often heard playing when no one is seated at it. One day a little boy pointed at the stairs and asked, "Who is that girl standing on the stairs?" No one else could see anyone there. Another time, a woman innocently told the Cumerlatos, "You know you have a ghost — she's standing beside the piano." Like the boy, the woman was the only person at the time who could see the forlorn ghost girl. A friend of Stephanie's was painting the staircase when a haunting face suddenly peered through the bannister with a sinister grin.

On another occasion, Stephanie's mother was helping her close the museum. It was late, they were all alone and it was pitch black. Stephanie remembered she had to feed Boris the tarantula some crickets, so they climbed up to the attic. After the task was done, they left Boris and Lizzie and made their way back down, but suddenly a powerful cold blast of air hit them head-on and Stephanie's mother gasped in fright. Stephanie assumed she had been startled by the inexplicable breeze. But that wasn't what had caused her fear. Her mother explained that someone had grabbed her hand and pinned it against the bannister. Stephanie then heard the disembodied voice of a young girl talking and laughing, as if the ghost was playing a practical joke.

One can only assume that Lizzie, sitting as still as a statue in the darkness above, might have winked in approval.

DON'T LET GO

Winnipeg, Manitoba

Everyone loves playing in the school playground during recess — everyone other than the children of St. Ignatius School. They avoid their school's rings at all costs. They know that to cross them is to cheat death or, more specifically, to cheat the girl who haunts their school's playground. And she's not a girl to be trifled with.

Not too long ago, a young boy approached the red rings with caution and a hint of fear. Although they weren't too high off the ground, a fall from that height coupled with an awkward landing could break a bone or twist an ankle.

A small crowd had formed around the boy to see if he'd make it across. He couldn't back down, not with so many eyes on him. The last thing the boy wanted was to be branded a coward, so he reached out a shaking, tentative hand and gripped the first ring. And then, swallowing his doubts and fears, he stepped off the ledge of the play structure, reached out his other hand and grabbed the second ring. Amazing even himself, he didn't fall. As he swung from ring to ring, his blood pumped harder and his smile grew wider. He was actually going to make it! But then, just when he reached the halfway point, someone grabbed his legs. He panicked and paused, struggling to hold on to the rings. The hands clawed up, up, up from his feet to his shins to his knees, pulling down as if trying to rip him free from the rings. The boy had to hold on with all his might and nearly lost his grip but, after summoning all his strength, was able to hang on tight and fend off whomever had tried to hurt him. He looked down and was shocked to see that there was no one beneath him.

Without wasting another second, the boy swung across the remaining rings and reached the safety of the other side. His friends were impressed and congratulated him for making it across, but he demanded to know who had tried to pull him down. His friends were dumbfounded. They hadn't seen anyone go near the boy.

Could the rumours be true? That was the only explanation the frightened boy and his equally frightened friends could think of. That a little ghost girl dwells on the playground with one simple mission in the afterlife: to pull children off the rings and to their deaths.

Legend has it that one day long ago, a kindergarten girl was attempting to cross the rings when her hand slipped and she fell. Tragically, her head struck one of the blue poles of the play structure with so much force that she died before she hit the ground. Unwilling to leave the scene of her death, the little girl hides in the playground's shadows and waits — and watches. Filled with jealousy

Rings much like those at St. Ignatius School

and seething with anger, she flies out of hiding and tries to pull others off the rings. But before anyone can get a good look at her, she disappears.

Opened in 1912 and run by the Sisters of the Holy Names of Jesus and Mary, the school has seen its fair share of challenges, from surviving the financial hardships of the Great Depression and the World Wars, to a 2007 electrical fire that burned down the oldest remaining wing of the building. But enrollment is high and the school is alive and well. Alive, except for the girl who would rather increase the playground's ghost population than see any children accomplish what she could not.

The children of St. Ignatius still warn each other to stay away from the red rings. And if someone is brave (or foolish) enough to try to cross them, the dire warning is clear and simple: whatever you do, don't let go.

AN IMAGINARY FRIEND

Montreal, Quebec

It's not uncommon for small children to have imaginary friends. When parents find their sons and daughters talking to an empty space, they know their child is simply going through a normal phase in life. There's certainly nothing unusual or creepy about it. Unless, of course, you one day begin to believe the supposed imaginary friend might not be imaginary after all — that the child is actually speaking and playing with someone from beyond the grave.

Newlyweds Kyle and Pete moved into their first home without any clue that something was amiss. It was the end unit of a row house on Georges-Vanier Street in Roxboro, a neighbourhood in Montreal. They were excited to start their married life together, and their heads were filled with dreams of what the future might hold. New experiences, new careers, children — it was very exhilarating. The house was admittedly small and ugly, but that didn't bother Kyle too much. It was all they could afford at the time, and she knew it wouldn't be their "forever home." But if she was being completely honest, there was something not quite right about the house on Georges-Vanier Street. Something she couldn't put her finger on. Even one of her best friends picked up on the bad vibe every time she visited. In fact, the friend hated coming over and told Kyle that she was certain there was some sort of presence in the house.

But life went on and they put such thoughts out of their minds. Soon they welcomed their first child, Gareth, into the world and brought him home. It was a happy time as Gareth grew and laughed and learned to crawl and walk and talk. And then, when Gareth was eighteen months old, something unusual began to happen.

Kyle found her son sitting on the bottom step of the staircase one day, looking up and talking to . . . something. Kyle looked upstairs, but no one was there. She asked Gareth who he was talking to.

"My friend," young Gareth replied. "Duke."

Kyle was surprised by the answer. Not only was this her son's first imaginary friend, but the name was unusual. Why Duke? They didn't know anyone named Duke and there weren't any Dukes in any of the books or shows they read and watched together.

The days passed and Gareth spent more and more time with Duke. "Come here, Duke," he would often say, leading his imaginary friend through the house. "Come with me, Duke." Often, when grown-ups would move to sit on the family room couch, Gareth would wave his arms wildly and yell, "Don't sit on Duke!" The bemused adults would willingly sit on the other side of the couch, looking at the empty spot beside them.

But was that spot actually as empty as the grown-ups believed? Kyle thought so, but her opinion would soon change.

One day while visiting with a neighbour who also lived on Georges-Vanier Street, Kyle casually mentioned that her son had an imaginary friend. As she elaborated and shared more details, her neighbour's eyes grew wider and wider. When Kyle revealed that the imaginary friend's name was Duke, her neighbour turned pale and finally spoke.

"Before you moved in, an old lady used to live in your home," the neighbour said softly with a slight quiver in her voice. "There was a fire. The old lady and her dog died in the blaze. The dog's name, Kyle. His name was Duke."

Everything suddenly made sense — bone-chilling, hair-raising sense. Gareth encouraging Duke to come down the stairs. Gareth patting his leg and telling Duke to "come with me." Gareth insisting that no one sit on Duke. His imaginary friend wasn't imaginary. He was a dog — a dead dog.

Gareth continued to talk and play with the ghost dog that only he could see until the day they moved out, when he was three years old. Gareth never saw Duke in their new house — the spirit had remained in the home where he had died — and Gareth never spoke of Duke again. In fact, now a grown-up, he no longer recalls having ever had an "imaginary" friend, ghost or no ghost. But his mother remembers only too well.

The next time you see a small child speaking to an empty corner of a room or an unoccupied chair, they might be playing with an imaginary friend. But it's also possible that the child might be making friends with an animal or person whose time on earth has come to an end, at least in the physical sense.

THE PIT OF DESPAIR

Dawson City, Yukon

The sky was grey and lifeless. The early morning sun was concealed behind a thick layer of clouds. The dirt road outside the Westminster Hotel was quiet. A figure walked alone.

The solitary figure was a mother who had come to see her son. He was a cleaner who worked the night shift at the Westminster Hotel. She walked slowly and hesitantly into the main floor lounge known as the Arm Pit and looked around. Not only was there no sign of her son, but she couldn't see another soul there. She called out. Her voice echoed across the room. No one replied. She slowly made her way deeper into the lounge. Then she heard something from the other side of the hotel.

The mother passed through a back passage that was

filled with dust, cobwebs and boilers, and approached a door to the bar, the Snake Pit. As she neared it, the sounds grew louder and became clearer. She could hear men's voices, talking, cajoling and laughing. And over the chatter was the distinctive clinking of poker chips. Had her son let his friends in for a game of cards when he was supposed to be working? The mother barged into the tavern and was met with the sight of another empty room. The sounds of the poker game, so clear when she was in the boiler room, stopped abruptly.

Wide, tall and painted baby pink, the Westminster Hotel has a bright and cheery face. But looks can be deceiving. Established in 1898 during the peak of the Klondike Gold Rush, the Pit, as locals affectionately call it, has seen its fair share of history.

Some of it has never left. Aaron Burnie, who works and lives in the Westminster Hotel, has witnessed no shortage of scary experiences he can't explain. He asserts that there is definitely "something" in the Pit, and he's not talking about the guests who visit the historic hotel to enjoy the rustic charm of its sloping ceilings and crooked floors. One night he awoke and needed to use the bathroom. All seemed normal until he made his way back to his room. Inexplicably, the hallway felt substantially colder, like he had entered a meat freezer. That gave him the creeps, but his next few experiences were far creepier.

After another trip to the second floor bathroom, Aaron was washing his hands when the locked door handle began rattling rapidly and loudly. Someone was trying to get in. "I'll just be a sec," Aaron called out. He quickly dried his hands, opened the door and found the hallway to be completely empty. Only three seconds had passed since someone had jiggled the handle. There was no possible way a living human being could have disappeared from the hallway so quickly.

Not long after, Aaron finally caught a glimpse of the ghost he had previously only felt and heard in the upstairs hallway — a man wearing a fedora hat, whom he'd see again and again, usually out of the corner of his eye. Others have seen him too, but that knowledge isn't necessarily comforting.

The spirit is protective of the lounge's piano. One day, when Aaron was relaxing in the Arm Pit, he saw a cellphone fly off the piano and across the room.

The Globe and Mail newspaper voted the Westminster Hotel the best venue in Canada for live music. If that's something you'd enjoy, you'll want to plan a visit soon. And if you prefer dead guests to live music, you also won't be disappointed.

TERMINUS OF THE DEAD

Vancouver, British Columbia

Experts believe that Waterfront Station might be the most haunted building in Vancouver, a city with such a bloody history that one of its streets is literally named Blood Alley. Built in 1915 by the Canadian Pacific Railway to serve the needs of a city that was growing rapidly, Waterfront Station was the Pacific terminus for trains travelling across the country from Montreal and Toronto. Since then, it has also become a terminus for the dead.

It's a grand building, built in a style reflective of the luxury and prestige that used to be synonymous with train travel. In its early days it contained accommodations for weary travellers as well as fine dining restaurants and a dance hall used for upper class parties and balls.

Today, some of these rooms are occupied by offices,

while others are used for storage, such as a room full of desks that have a habit of silently moving on their own.

On a dark, cold night, a security guard working the night shift prowled through the wide, empty halls of Waterfront Station. His footfalls echoed off the stone walls as he swung his flashlight from side to side. He was alone, or so he thought, as he entered one of the building's storage rooms. In order to search the room he had to swivel his large frame around the old desks that were stored there. When the guard reached the back of the room, he turned and was paralyzed with fear. The desks had silently floated off the ground and repositioned themselves. Some blocked the door while others were piled in the middle of the floor, forming a crude blockade that had cut him off from his only means of escape. Not only was he trapped, but he couldn't comprehend how that had happened.

There was only one explanation: the ghostly tales of Waterfront Station his co-workers had shared were true. A ghost — or perhaps a host of ghosts — had ensnared him in the room. But for what purpose? The security guard didn't wait around to find out. He ran full speed toward the desks, leapt up on the nearest one and sprinted across them to the door, eager to put the haunted room as far behind him as quickly as possible.

Between 2004 and 2005, a guard heard phantom footsteps in a stairwell on three separate occasions. The first time it happened the feet approached so quickly and unexpectedly that the guard barely had time to think before the sound ran past within half a metre of him. The second time he was a little more prepared and stood in mute horror as the sound of someone running passed by, once again without a visible body. The third time the guard was not alone. He was with a colleague who also

Waterfront Station

heard the footsteps, proving to him that the sound was not a product of his imagination.

One night, a different guard wandered toward the west side of the building where the dance hall used to be located. As he got closer, he slowed his pace. He heard something. It was faint at first, but it grew louder as he approached. It was the sound of music from the 1920s. That didn't make sense; the station's sound system wasn't connected. When the guard finally entered the old ballroom the music was so loud he thought he had just stepped back in time and into the middle of a swinging party. At first the room appeared to be empty. But then, out of the corner of his eye, he spotted a solitary figure: a woman, dressed in a 1920s flapper dress, waltzing alone across the floor in time with the music. The guard took a step toward the woman, but suddenly the music stopped and the woman vanished on the spot.

On another occasion, a guard opened a door and walked into a dark storage room, completely unprepared to come face to face with the old woman staring back at him. She glowed bright white and had a look of sadness and pain etched upon her face. The woman floated and reached her hand out to him, which sent him running in the opposite direction.

Others have also rounded a corner to find three women sitting on a bench as if waiting for a midnight train. Like the dancing spectre, they disappear almost as soon as they've been spotted.

And it's not only security guards who have seen ghosts in Waterfront Station. Many employees who work in the offices have had their fair share of unwanted paranormal encounters. Debra Lummas, a senior account executive, recalls the time she was speaking with another employee in one of the bathrooms when a third woman suddenly and creepily joined them. The stranger had wavy brown hair that flowed over her shoulders and wore a glamorous blue blouse from a different time period. She stared silently at Debra for an awkward ten seconds, then whispered in an ethereal voice, "I'll come back another time," and promptly vanished.

And finally, no account of the spirits of Waterfront Station would be complete without the Headless Brakeman who has been seen prowling on the tracks. On a night in 1928, as the rain was coming down in sheets, an unfortunate CPR brakeman named Hub Clark was working outside when he slipped and landed on his head. The fall rendered him unconscious and he lay sprawled across the tracks. A passenger train sped toward him before Clark regained consciousness, and he didn't see it coming. His head was cut clean from his body. It wasn't long before other CPR employees began seeing Clark step out of the shadows on misty nights, a lantern held high in the air. He walks up and down the tracks through the dead hours, forever searching for his missing head.

Last stop, Waterfront Station. End of the line. It's time to get off the train. But if it's late and you have a bad feeling in your gut, no one would blame you for wanting to stay on the train a little longer. Some of Waterfront Station's travellers have yet to reach their final destination.

THE LIVING MUSEUM

Edmonton, Alberta

The Karpetz family purchased a beautiful home on Saskatchewan Drive and decided to spruce it up a little before moving in. Named the Firkins House after the original owner, it was well known to neighbours as the dwelling of some dark presence. But the Karpetzes had no idea. Soon — very soon — they would.

Shortly after taking possession of the possessed house, Audrey Karpetz worked late into the night painting one of the upstairs bedrooms. However, the spirit that inhabited the home's walls must not have appreciated the change in decor. Exhausted but satisfied with the day's work, Audrey, alone in the house, switched off the upstairs light and turned to leave. As she approached the top of the stairs, she was suddenly grabbed from behind in a tight and frigid embrace. She fought free from whatever had latched on to her body and ran outside as quickly as she could.

When she found the courage to look back at the house, she saw that the upstairs lights had turned back on. The rational part of her brain calmed her fears and reminded her that she had been alone. The logical explanation was that her mind was playing tricks on her. She must have imagined the touch of the hands and accidentally left the lights on in her haste to get out. She must have.

Filled with newfound (but slightly shaky) confidence, Audrey walked back into the house and up the stairs. She switched off the light and turned to leave.

Something grabbed her from the darkness, just as before.

This time, Audrey didn't try to convince herself it was only her imagination. The embrace of the hands was far too real. She screamed and ran out of the house. Once outside she saw that, much to her horror, the upstairs light had once again turned back on. She locked the door and left. Upon returning the next morning, Audrey and her husband Rod found that the upstairs light had been turned off at some point during the night.

The Karpetzes still moved into the house as planned, hoping the ghostly encounters would stop. They didn't.

Late one night, Audrey returned home with her two young daughters. She tucked the sleeping girls into their beds and went downstairs to the kitchen. There, sitting at the table like he owned the place, was an old man she didn't recognize. After overcoming her initial fright, Audrey asked the man what he was doing in her house. She assumed he must be a friend of her husband's or a neighbour she hadn't yet had the opportunity to meet, but the man didn't answer. She rubbed her eyes and when she looked at the table again the man had disappeared without a trace.

In 1992, Rod and Audrey Karpetz sold the house, and it was transported to the Fort Edmonton Park, Canada's largest living museum. Located along the North Saskatchewan River, the park takes visitors through time, from the Fur Trade Era, the Settlement Era, the Municipal Era to the Metropolitan Era. Throughout the summer, the park is filled with costumed historical interpreters who interact with visitors, and for a once-in-a-lifetime experience the Hotel Selkirk is fully operational, allowing people to stay in the park overnight.

Interior of the Firkins House

The legend of the haunted house in the living museum has grown over the years, making it hard to decipher the truth. People have reported seeing a transparent woman floating near a bookcase in the study, even claiming to have captured her in pictures. Others tell the story of a previous owner who repeatedly found a creepy ventriloquist's doll that turned up in odd places throughout the house as if it had a life of its own. Listen closely in one of the upstairs bedrooms that used to be a nursery and you might hear a disembodied voice singing lullabies as if to soothe a baby. And many people have reported seeing a boy running through the halls, bouncing a red ball in such a carefree manner that it seems he doesn't even know he's dead. There are so many reputable people who have seen odd phenomena that the reports are impossible to ignore.

Take, for example, the workers who were tasked with the building's restoration and installation in Fort Edmonton Park. Their tools kept disappearing and reappearing in bizarre spots as if they had grown legs. A windowpane flew out of a second-floor window frame and, despite being glass, didn't shatter or crack when it hit the ground below. It seemed like it had been guided softly down to the ground. It made no sense.

A security guard who worked the night shift in the park for years had countless odd experiences when he was, presumably, all alone. He says that once the spirits got to know him he was mostly left alone. His two most vivid (and chilling) memories from within the Firkins House include one night when he saw a chair slide from one side of a room to the other, and another night when he was pushed violently from behind.

Have you decided whether or not you'd want to spend a

night in the Hotel Selkirk, so close to the Firkins House? Well, before you book a room, consider this. A tourist who stayed overnight wandered through the park after it had closed and filmed the historic buildings. Nothing seemed out of the ordinary . . . at the time. But when he reviewed the footage a few days after his trip, he couldn't believe what he had captured. The video showed that he was alone in the middle of the moonlit street. The camera was focused on the Firkins House. And then a faint voice clearly whispered, *"Come see . . ."* followed by the piercing squawk of a crow.

The choice is yours. Visit Fort Edmonton Park during the day, or spend a night sleeping beside one of the country's most haunted houses. It's sure to be a night you'll never forget.

THE CRISIS APPARITION

Sydney, Nova Scotia

Winter came early to the colony of Cape Breton Island in 1785. It was October 15, yet Sydney Harbour was already frozen, delaying the delivery from England of much needed supplies that the 33rd Regiment of Foot were expecting. The British soldiers were holed up in their barracks as snow piled up outside their doors and their windows froze over with crackling ice.

The men were prisoners to the severe weather and passed their time playing cards and trying not to succumb to the madness of cabin fever and isolation that threatened to crush them under its weight. It was in the midst of this dire situation that Captain John Coape Sherbrooke would look upon the face of his friend, Lieutenant George West Wynyard, and become filled with dread. "I have heard,"

Sherbrooke would later remark, "of a man's being as pale as death, but I never saw a living face assume the appearance of a corpse, except Wynyard's at that moment."

On the night in question, between 8 and 9 p.m., Sherbrooke and Wynyard sat before a warm fire discussing literature and ideologies while drinking coffee. They weren't interested in gambling nor were they alcohol drinkers, so they spent many evenings in Wynyard's parlour, apart from the other soldiers. There were only two doors in the sitting room: one leading to the barracks's hallway and the other to Wynyard's bedroom. As they passed the time in conversation, Sherbrooke happened to glance at the doorway that led to the hall. Standing in it was a man he had never seen before.

This man was young and tall but looked very ill. He was as pale as frost and emaciated, looking as if he hadn't eaten in days, or even weeks. The mysterious man was not dressed in a military uniform but in a hunting suit. He held a whip in his hand.

Sherbrooke alerted Wynyard to the stranger. As soon as Wynyard laid eyes on the intruder he became incredibly agitated and his face took on the appearance of a corpse, as Sherbrooke would later describe. Wynyard couldn't move, couldn't speak. So the two men looked at the third in stony silence. Finally, after an uncomfortable pause that felt like a lifetime, the stranger crossed the room, looked at Wynyard with deep sadness and pain, and then walked into the bedroom, out of sight.

Wynyard drew in a gasp of air as if he hadn't breathed for a few minutes — in truth, he probably hadn't — and then grasped Sherbrooke's arm. "Great God!" he exclaimed. "My brother!" As far as Wynyard was aware, his brother Jack was home in England.

Failing to understand how Wynyard's brother could be in Cape Breton, and certain Wynyard must be mistaken, Sherbrooke led his friend into the bedroom to ask the stranger who he was. But the small room — including the closet — was completely empty. *Impossible*, Sherbrooke thought. There were no other doors and the windows were sealed shut with ice. The men took their search back into the parlour and even examined the hallway but found no trace of Wynyard's brother. He had disappeared. They took note of the time at which the emaciated man had first appeared and made a pact not to tell any of the other men for fear of creating a stir.

But Wynyard was distraught. He thought that something bad had happened, that some tragedy had befallen his brother, and that the haunting vision that had walked through his sitting room was a bad omen.

Time passed but his anxiety did not. He grew increasingly impatient for the next shipment of letters from England, hoping to hear his brother was okay, and he began to confide in his comrades that he feared his brother might not be well. The other men in the 33rd Regiment became suspicious. Finally, after prolonged prodding, Wynyard shared the story of his brother's appearance in the night.

The men quickly became obsessed with the tale and were determined — perhaps nearly as much as Wynyard himself — to discover what had happened. They searched newspapers from England for any notice of the Wynyard name and anxiously awaited the next delivery of letters from home. When the mail finally arrived, all the men demanded to know if Wynyard had received a letter before they asked for their own long-awaited correspondence from home. But no letter had come for Wynyard. The men, disappointed, dispersed.

There was, however, a solitary letter addressed to Sherbrooke. He stood staring at it for some time and then finally turned it over, broke the seal and opened it. After a quick glance at its contents, Sherbrooke asked Wynyard to follow him to a private room. They left.

Silence filled the mailroom. The soldiers were convinced Sherbrooke's letter contained some clue — perhaps the full explanation — to the appearance of Wynyard's brother earlier in the year.

After an hour had passed and the suspense had become nearly unbearable, Sherbrooke finally returned. He crossed the room without speaking or making eye contact with anyone and stopped at the fireplace. He rested his arm and head on the mantel and stared deep into the flames. After another agonizingly drawn-out moment, he said in a low whisper that only those closest to him could hear, "Wynyard's brother is no more."

The letter had begun: "Dear John, Break to your friend,

New settlement on the Island of Cape Breton, 1785

Wynyard, the death of his favourite brother." It further explained, Sherbrooke relayed with a chill, that Jack had died on October 15 at the exact time that the ghost — for by now the men had come to believe that the emaciated stranger must surely have been a ghost — had walked into Wynyard's parlour and looked forlornly at his brother.

But Jack Wynyard was no simple ghost. He was what's known as a crisis apparition — the spirit of a person who appears before loved ones at the time of death.

Why Jack's spirit travelled halfway around the world and walked past his brother without a word before disappearing is unknown. But forty years later, while speaking with a friend, Sherbrooke solemnly swore that the story was completely true. That night had made him a changed man who looked on matters of life, death and eternity in a different light, and he believed he'd soon be called into another world himself. Whether or not he returned after death is unknown.

AFRAID OF THE DARKE

Regina, Saskatchewan

In the late 1800s, Francis Nicholson Darke was a successful businessman and landowner. He was also mayor of Regina, a member of parliament and donated much of the money needed to build the University of Regina. As a supporter of the performing arts, he funded the construction of the Darke Hall for Music and Art on the campus. He died in 1940, but that hasn't stopped him from enjoying the performances in the building named for him.

During musical programs, modern-day audiences have spotted a man sitting in the middle of the auditorium who stands out from the crowd. He's well dressed in a suit that resembles the style that was popular in the early 1900s, and he always sits alone. He doesn't speak to anyone nor seem to even be aware of his surroundings, utterly transfixed by the music performed on stage. When the music ends and the audience stands to applaud, the man disappears.

Darke has also been seen in other locations about campus. Dana Hryhoriw, who would later form a paranormal research team, saw her first ghost standing on the steps outside Darke Hall. She locked eyes with the man and immediately felt like a thousand volts of electricity had surged through her body and taken her breath away. Wanting to learn more about whom the man might have been, she went to the library and began flipping through the pages of local history books. She turned to a picture

Francis Nicholson Darke (back row, second from right)
Regina Town Council, 1896

of Darke from the 1930s and knew at once it was the man she had seen. It was as if he was looking out at her intently from within the picture.

Terry Duckett, a technician with the university's music department, recalls with uneasiness an odd occurrence that took place every night for three weeks. Whenever he was alone in the evening he felt a powerful draft of cold air pouring down from the ceiling near his office. There were no vents nearby and he checked to make sure all the building's doors and windows were closed. Finally, things grew too scary for Terry and — although he doesn't know why — he said, "Good night, Frank," as he was locking up. The cold air immediately turned to warm air, and Terry ran from the building.

Are you afraid of the dark? If one day you enroll for classes at the University of Regina, you might be wise to develop a healthy fear of the Darke.

THE HAUNTiNG OF HiLLCREST HOUSE

St. Catharines, Ontario

It's a beautiful home on an idyllic street in Ontario's historic Garden City. But beauty can be deceiving, and something dark and sinister dwells within the house on Hillcrest Avenue.

Lindsay was a teenager when her family moved in. With many windows, white pillars and a red door, the home had a pleasant, welcoming face. Large, mature trees grew on the property and green bushes filled the garden, creating a warm and healthy appearance that made the house instantly feel like home.

Once they had unpacked, Lindsay, her sister and their two brothers began exploring every nook and cranny. One of the house's interesting quirks was the attic. It wasn't the type you'd see in a horror movie, with dust-covered knick-knacks and cobwebs in every corner. Instead, it was a finished and functional living space with a sitting room at one end and a bedroom at the other. Lindsay and her siblings discovered that there was a secret passage joining the sitting room and bedroom. It was exciting and mysterious, but it also felt . . . wrong. Lindsay had the feeling that she was being watched in the attic, whether she was with her siblings or alone. With the sickening sensation of eyes on her back, she'd spin around — but nothing was ever there.

The secret tunnel also had a secret of its own. Set into one of the walls was a hidden cubbyhole that the kids stumbled upon one day. They opened it, reached into the darkness and pulled out, much to their surprise, a German army helmet from the World War I era. Called a *pickelhaube*, the helmet was made of black polished leather and had a large metal spike sticking straight up from its top. Lindsay and her siblings were filled with curiosity and a touch of fear as they passed the spiked helmet among them, wondering what horrors the helmet had seen. And how had it ended up in a hidden cubbyhole, in a secret tunnel, in the attic of their home? They returned the helmet to its hiding place and tried to put it out of their minds.

But as strange and creepy as the attic was, nothing could match the feeling of fear that filled the house's library on the main floor.

It was a long room situated in the back of the house and running the entire length of the main floor. The family filled it with books and cozy wing chairs perfect for reading. Their television sat in a corner, and it was their preferred room for socializing and relaxing. But Lindsay's sister admitted that she felt like she was always being watched by an unseen presence in the library, just as Lindsay had felt in the attic. That didn't keep them out of the room, but it did stop several dogs from entering. Oddly, no dog ever set foot in the library. Instead, they put on their brakes and went ramrod straight outside the room's doorway. With bristling hair and bared teeth, the dogs whined incessantly, a pitiful sound of terror and agitation. The dogs' instincts were clear: there was something bad in the library, whether the humans could see it or not.

Early one morning, Lindsay's mother woke up and walked downstairs. She was often the first person in the household to rise, and she passed from room to room tidying and getting ready for the day. The house was silent, empty. Nothing seemed unusual or out of place, until she entered the library.

All of the books had been taken down from the shelves and were laid out on the floor in the shape of a star. Wondering who had created the mess, she picked up the books and returned them to the shelves. She might have forgotten the unusual occurrence had it been an isolated event, but it happened again. Another morning she came down to find the books on the floor in the shape of the letter H. Again she cleaned them up thinking that would be the last time, but she found them another morning arranged in a series of large squares, and a few days later in perfectly spaced rows.

She was convinced that the children were playing a practical joke on her, sneaking downstairs in the dark to lay out all the books, but each child insisted she or he was not to blame. Possessing the uncanny ability mothers have to know immediately when one of her children is telling a lie, she knew that her kids were telling the truth. But the books continued to move during the night and form perfect geometrical patterns on the floor.

Despite the dogs' refusal to enter the room and a shared and growing feeling amongst the family that the library was haunted, no one saw or felt a presence within. That was about to change.

Late one night, Lindsay was home alone. The house was dark. Every sound — the wind blowing a tree branch against a window, the tick-tock of an old clock, the creaks and groans of the wood floors — was amplified by the silence. Lindsay decided to sit and rest in one of the library's wing chairs, a choice she'd soon regret. An eerie sensation washed over Lindsay, and goosebumps prickled her skin. With a sickening lurch in her stomach, she suddenly believed there was someone directly behind her. She turned swiftly and looked over her shoulder, but no one was in the space between her chair and the wall.

She turned back around, but before another second passed a hand grabbed her left shoulder from behind. She tensed and froze, her breath catching in the back of her throat. Lindsay could make out the distinct feeling of four fingers and a thumb on her flesh and bone. It was not a comforting pat, the sort of gesture a loved one would give. It was something evil, something cruel. After a short moment that felt like an eternity, the hand pressed down on her hard, pinning her to the chair. And then, as suddenly as it had touched her, it let go. Lindsay turned again but saw only her own reflection in a window looking back at her. She screamed, leapt out of the chair and ran out of the library. She sought out the company and security of her dogs, went into the kitchen and turned on the radio for a distraction as she waited for her family to return.

Many years have passed since Lindsay and her family moved out of Hillcrest House, but they'll never forget the *pickelhaube*, the mystery of the rearranging books and the hand that squeezed Lindsay's shoulder one night. Memories may fade, but fear is forever.

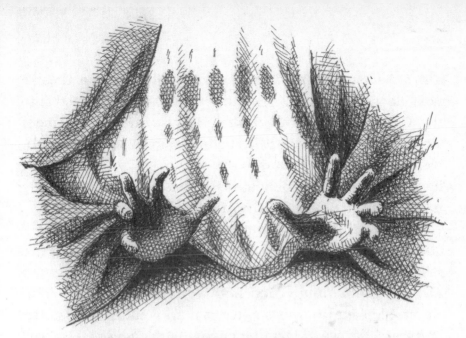

WHERE THE DEAD TAKE CENTRE STAGE

Moncton, New Brunswick

The historic Capitol Theatre has a 782-seat auditorium, but one of those seats is spoken for. Permanently.

In 2014, Lindsay Isenor and a few friends took a tour of the theatre, which has been designated as a Provincial Historic Site. When she stepped onto the stage and took in the decadent beauty of the two-storey auditorium her jaw dropped. She was speechless. Although this emotional reaction was completely natural given the splendor of the theatre, she would soon experience similarly intense reactions created by decidedly unnatural forces.

Lindsay's tour of the Capitol included a stop in the lobby where she saw an old black and white photograph of Alexander "Sandy" Lindsay. Below Alexander's picture was a plaque that told his tragic story. On March 26, 1926, a fire devastated the Capitol and the Empress, a theatre next door. Alexander, a volunteer firefighter, rushed into the Capitol to fight the blaze. He was in the basement when the stage collapsed, crushing him beneath the rubble. To this day he remains the only on-duty firefighter to have lost his life in Moncton. He also remains, according to present-day staff, the theatre's resident ghost.

After Lindsay and the tour group crossed the catwalk above the stage and saw the original brick walls that are still charred from the fire, an employee told the group about a frightening vision he'd witnessed late one night. He had looked up and spotted a man walking across the balcony. That was alarming enough since no one else was supposed to have been in the theatre. The truly scary part was that the stranger was not bothering to walk *around* the seats, but was walking straight *through* them.

Feeling excited and a little anxious from this story, Lindsay and her friend Dave investigated the balcony alone. They sat in one of the rows and waited, hoping to experience their own fright. They soon got their wish.

One of the seats directly behind them began to squeak as if someone seated there was moving side to side to get a better view of the stage. They spun around, but all of the chairs were empty. Then, from the same empty seat where they had heard movement, a man began to laugh. Whether the ghost was laughing at a performance only he could see or at the startled looks on Lindsay and Dave's faces, no one could say. But they were determined to find out who the ghost was, so they asked, "What is your name?"

"Alex," said a gruff, moaning voice.

Lindsay and Dave confirmed that they had both heard the ghostly response, and then a whistle sounded three times from the stage — *fweet, fweet, fweet* — as if in reply to Alex's voice.

Later, when Lindsay and Dave rejoined their friends, Charmian and Dwayne, they asked if anyone on the main level had whistled. No one had.

The group agreed they could all use a break. While they sat on the stage and chatted, Lindsay noticed that a door she had propped open and secured with a stop wedge was now closed. She asked if anyone had closed the door. Everyone shook their heads. She rewound through the footage on a camera that she had set up on a tripod onstage. The open door could be seen in the back of the frame. With the soft blue light of the camera's screen illuminating her face, Lindsay watched the odd scene in horror: a moment after the group passed through the doorway, the stop wedge flew out from under the door. The door swung shut, missing the last person in the party by mere inches, but somehow didn't make a sound. It was like a scene out of a horror movie, and the friends had unwittingly become the terrorized characters.

Charmian and Dwayne, sensing that the paranormal activity in the theatre was growing in intensity, ventured into the basement where the collapsed stage had claimed Alexander's life many years ago. A short while later, Dwayne fled from the basement and rejoined the others. They could tell something was bothering him and asked what had happened. He told them that he and Charmian had brought along an Ovilus, a device that reads electromagnetic frequencies and changes in temperature, then feeds the data into a preset database of over two thousand words, allowing spirits to communicate with the living. When they turned on the Ovilus three words came through:

273

Bury
Under
Burn

The temperature then immediately plummeted and Dwayne was overwhelmed with an odd sense of dark energy, forcing him to leave.

It's clear that Lindsay and her friends were joined by the ghost of Alexander that night. But for them, it was an isolated event. For the Capitol's staff, working with the spirit is an all-too-familiar aspect of the job.

Kimberley Rayworth, Development Director at the theatre, says that almost every member of staff has felt Al's presence, including her.

It was Christmas day, and all was quiet and calm. Although the theatre was closed, someone had to stop by the empty building to make sure the pipes hadn't frozen. That someone was Kim. Luckily she didn't have to go in alone. She happened to be dog-sitting for one of the theatre's regular performers, so she took Norman the dog along with her for company.

Kim and Norman walked through the quiet building, the sound of their feet and paws echoing in the empty rooms. All seemed well. No frozen pipes, no other emergencies. She was almost ready to lock up and return home when something unexpected and unsettling happened.

They were in a conference room located under the second floor balcony — under Alexander's seat. Without warning, an awful feeling of not being alone overwhelmed Kim. Norman grew really quiet and dropped uncomfortably low to the ground. Suddenly, the silence was shattered by the sound of heavy fireman's boots running across the floor above her head. The hair on her arms and neck stood on end and her body grew painfully cold. Kim's

Stage in the Capitol Theatre

mind went instantly to Alexander — somehow, she knew he was in the building with her, perhaps looking for a little company over the holidays.

Julie Pallot, the theatre's Guest Services Manager, was leading a tour for a local class of ten- to twelve-year-old students when she had her own paranormal experience. She led the kids to the stage and stood with her back to the curtain while she shared the theatre's history and told them about the resident ghost. As Julie began to suspect that the kids didn't really believe a spirit haunted the old building, a teacher standing beside her on the stage suddenly screamed loudly. The teacher clamped her mouth shut and didn't say what had scared her, but her face was pale and a look of fear had overcome her. She looked like she had seen a ghost. As Julie would soon find out, the teacher hadn't seen a ghost — she had *felt* one.

Not wanting to embarrass the teacher in front of the

students, Julie waited until they were alone before she asked what had happened. With a pinched mouth, a shake of her head and a look of repulsion, the teacher said that while Julie spoke to the class, someone had grabbed her leg from behind. And then fingers had squeezed her tightly.

There hadn't been anyone near them — no one *living*, that is. To this day, Julie never stands in front of the curtain while speaking to groups. She sits on the edge of the stage, a safe distance from the curtain. She has no desire to be grabbed by a cold, dead hand.

In the Capitol Theatre there are two types of shows that take place on its historic stage: live performances and dead ones.

GHOST HiLL

Luskville, Quebec

In the 1940s, a farmer named Wyman McKechnie was out walking under a large moon in a clouded sky. Whenever the clouds blew in front of the moon McKechnie found it difficult to see much further than a few feet, but when the clouds parted he happened to look over his shoulder. There, standing in the middle of the road on Ghost Hill, was the shadowy shape of a man in a white cloak, floating a foot above the ground. Terrified, McKechnie yelled and quickened his pace. The ghost behind matched his speed. McKechnie broke out into a run and the ghost followed suit. McKechnie sprinted but still he couldn't lose his pursuer. He ran until he was forced to sit on a log to catch his breath.

The ghost glided to the other end of the log and said in a whisper, "Well, we were certainly going some there."

McKechnie jumped to his feet and found the courage to respond, "Yes! And now that I've got my breath we'll go some more!" He beat the ghost back to his home, but he couldn't outrun the nightmares that plagued his sleep thereafter.

Today, Highway 148 runs through Luskville, up and over Ghost Hill. The only buildings on Ghost Hill are a small stone church that's built so close to the road it's practically in the middle of it, and an old farmhouse tucked out of sight on a hidden lane. The bush that grows on both sides of the road is tangled and oppressive, and the road itself is steep and winding. There have been many fatal accidents on this stretch of road over the years. Some blame the road. Others blame the ghosts.

In the early 1800s, a young man stalked silently through the woods with a shotgun in hand. He was hoping to catch a partridge or two for his evening meal. The sky was unnaturally dark and gloomy, casting a lifeless grey light on his surroundings that made it very difficult to see.

As the man began to climb a hill, he saw a cow at the top lumbering slowly down toward him. The man stopped and regarded the cow; it looked odd in the dying light. Something wasn't quite right. And then the cow suddenly began to charge the man, running in a very peculiar fashion. The man had a bad feeling in his gut. He raised his rifle and, when the cow had covered half the distance, he pulled the trigger. A loud bang echoed over the hills. The cow toppled over right beside an old, gnarled tree. The man ran to it and looked down in horror. The cow he thought he had shot turned out to be another man — his best friend, in fact — who had put on a cow's hide to frighten his buddy. It worked, all right. And the practical joker paid for the gag with his life.

But his soul could not pass on. It's believed his spirit left his still-warm body and fused into the tree. The branches looked like bony, many-fingered arms, the roots like knobbly legs stuck in the muck and the bark like the folded wrinkles of a face that has seen too much pain and misery. The hill where the tree stood became known as Ghost Hill.

The haunted tree wasn't content to become a forgotten part of the landscape. Instead, it became the source of much mischief, enacting revenge on unsuspecting and unfortunate travellers who happened by. Terrified farmers abandoned their wagons and rushed to the safety of their homes, telling their families that the wheels had seized in the middle of Ghost Hill as if some unseen force had reached out and ensnared them in its mighty grasp. Horses commonly became agitated and spooked, seemingly at nothing, and kicked up on their hind legs, dropping their drivers to the ground and bolting away in the night. Men who found themselves without a horse would get up, brush the dirt off their pants and suddenly hear eerie sounds like whispers that grew to howls in the woods all around them. No one stayed long to find out what made those uncanny noises in the dark.

Something had to be done about the haunted tree. And so, in 1830, the task of chopping it down fell to the man who owned the land, an Irish immigrant and farmer named Joseph Lusk.

Mad with fear and laughing hysterically, Joseph Lusk hacked away at the base of the gnarled tree. Lightning flashed and illuminated Lusk's wide eyes as he threw himself at his fevered task, pausing only briefly now and again to wipe sweat out of his eyes and brush wood chips off his coat. With every gouge he cut in the tree he could swear he

Ghost Hill Farm

heard an anguished scream. It was as if he wasn't chopping down a tree, but hacking a human to bits. In a dark, twisted sense, that wasn't too far from the truth.

When the work was done, the townsfolk hoped they would no longer see another ghost. But a few short years later, Ghost Hill claimed another innocent victim.

A couple of men were returning home late at night from a tavern in nearby Aylmer when they broke out into an argument. The friends had fought before, as friends do, and their disagreements were normally resolved and quickly forgotten. This time, however, one of the men reached into the back of his horse-drawn wagon, pulled out a pitchfork and impaled his friend upon the metal prongs, right at the top of Ghost Hill. The murdered man's spirit took up permanent residence in the woods.

In 1885, a local farmer by the name of Jim Boyer had a profitable day at the Aylmer market, selling butter, pork and vegetables. He rode home happy, his pockets heavy with profits, when a band of robbers ambushed him on Ghost Hill, stole his money and left him to die in a puddle of his own blood. Boyer's soul joined the multiplying group of hilltop ghosts forever wailing for justice against their murderers but never finding peace.

It's believed other spirits skulk through the woods of Ghost Hill, and in the 1930s one of these ghosts hitched a ride on a bus as it drove along Highway 148. As the driver crested the hill, he happened to steal a glance in the rear-view mirror. He had thought the bus was empty, so he was shocked to see an elderly woman sitting in one of the back rows, looking solemnly out the window. As he drove down the other side of the hill, he wondered how he hadn't seen her get on the bus. He decided he should pull over at the bottom of the hill to let her out. As he passed a small cemetery he heard a loud *whoosh* — as if something had flown straight past him, through the closed door and out into the night. The driver stopped the bus, opened the door and turned around . . . but the bus was empty once again.

Sometimes a name is only a name, nothing more. But Ghost Hill is more than that. It's a dire warning of what you'll find if you're brave enough to venture through Luskville.

SPIRITS IN THE SANATORIUM

Fort Qu'Appelle, Saskatchewan

As the teenage musicians gathered outside the building where their summer band camp was being held, on the grounds of what was once the Fort Qu'Appelle Sanatorium, it suddenly dawned on one of the young men that he had forgotten something. But what? He had his case, his instrument . . . *My sheet music!* he suddenly remembered. He had left it in his room. He told his bandmates he'd return and raced back to their lodge alone. The boy ran up the stairs and into his room where he picked up his music . . . and paused.

He had heard something. He thought he was the only person currently in the building, which had been assigned to the boys. A soft, lilting voice was coming from the bathroom, singing beautifully. The voice clearly belonged to a woman.

As he hesitantly approached the bathroom, the woman's voice grew louder and clearer. It was accompanied by the sound of running water. He stood in the hallway for a moment, listening to the woman's song and building up the nerve to investigate further. Finally he cracked open the door.

The woman continued singing. Her back was to the boy. She wore a long, old-fashioned dress and was washing her hands in the sink as she sang.

With a dry swallow, the boy said, "Excuse me? Lady? I think you are in the wrong lodge."

She didn't stop singing, she didn't stop washing and she didn't acknowledge the boy in any way. It was as if she was in her own world. The boy would soon realize that she was, quite literally, in her own world — a parallel world.

But then she stopped singing abruptly and turned off the taps. She stood statue-still and didn't turn around. All he could see was her back. The sudden silence was deafening, nerve-wracking. Finally, she backed away from the sink and out of sight.

The boy stepped into the bathroom and looked around the corner, but it was empty. The woman had disappeared. He looked more closely at the sink. It was completely dry.

The boy knew he had seen a ghost singing and washing in the bathroom; the only question was which one? There is no shortage of spectres roaming Fort San's haunted halls.

The most well-known is Nurse Jane, a woman who is said to have become so distraught from treating hundreds of sick and dying patients that she ended her life. She's often seen in her white uniform and cap, wandering the halls pushing a squeaky, empty wheelchair, with a morose, downcast glance.

Others have seen the ghosts of children running through the buildings and outside in the woods, some laughing, some crying. Many have been woken in the middle of the night by the sounds of beds being dragged across the floor, chains rattling above, hushed voices in the dark, and windows and doors opening and closing on their own.

Fort Qu'Appelle Sanatorium, or Fort San, was opened on October 10, 1917, to treat patients with tuberculosis. At its peak as a tuberculosis sanatorium, Fort San was so large that it produced its own power and grew its own crops. It was virtually self-contained, with a school, canteen, barber shop, post office, movie theatre, library and internal radio station. It also had a morgue, of course. Unclaimed bodies were carted out of the main building and buried in unmarked graves in a small cemetery nestled in the woods.

As tuberculosis cases dwindled, so did the need for sanatoriums, and Fort San was closed on April 1, 1971. The property was then used as a summer school for the arts and a conference centre.

It's rumoured that years after the sanatorium closed the new owners discovered that the entrances to the tunnels that connected all of the buildings and the morgue had been sealed shut. They pried them open and were horrified to find hundreds of dried and shrivelled bodies underground. It's little wonder there are so many stories of ghostly encounters.

One night a man named Pat was trying to sleep when someone grabbed his hand and checked his wrist for a pulse. When Pat opened his eyes, he saw that his hand was raised in the air and there were finger indents on his skin. But no one stood beside him. The ghost finished

Fort Qu'Appelle Sanatorium

checking Pat's vitals and placed his hand back down on his chest. Pat couldn't bear the thought of spending one more night there and left.

Since 2004 the buildings have sat unused, slowly crumbling and falling into disrepair. The fields are overgrown and the cemetery has been reclaimed by nature. This seems to please the spirits just fine.

A man named Dieter explored the abandoned property with three friends, two of whom grew too scared and had to wait outside one of the buildings. Dieter and the friend who remained with him searched every single room, from the top floors to the lowly basement. Once they were certain that they were the only living beings inside, they knocked on the walls and called upon spirits to knock back in response. A silent second passed, then another, a third and finally they heard a reply: *knock, knock, knock.*

That was enough for Dieter and his friend, and they quickly ran out of the building. They rejoined their two friends outside, where they saw through the windows orb-like lights zipping up and down the halls. It was absolutely terrifying, and they ran off the property, never to return.

More recently, a woman took her Rottweiler-Doberman mix, a large and powerful dog she described as "afraid of nothing," to explore the abandoned sanatorium. As soon as they arrived, the dog ran through the main building's open door. She waited outside for ten minutes, too afraid to move and hoping her dog would return. She couldn't hear the dog running or barking, and she finally grew too concerned to wait outside any longer. She walked in, up the stairs, down the hall and finally found the dog. He was alone in an empty room, standing ramrod straight, staring at an empty corner. He didn't respond when his name was called. Suddenly something imperceptible happened. The dog broke out of his trance-like state and ran out of the room, shooting past his owner in a blind panic. He tore around the building in a frenzy, running back and forth down halls, up and down the stairs and around and around in circles within rooms. He was like "a rabbit running away from a wolf," as the woman described. After ten minutes she finally managed to get him back outside, where the dog immediately returned to his normal self. What was in the corner of that room? Only the dog will ever know.

One thing is certain: every corner of Fort San seems to be haunted, be it by floating light orbs, a sombre nurse or a singing spectre.

NIGHTMARE HOUSE

St. John's, Newfoundland and Labrador

Taking their first steps into their new home on Queen's Road, the young family who purchased the old three-storey row house were excited and happy. But what they hoped would be their dream house quickly became a nightmare.

As soon as they set foot inside, everyone was over-come by an unsettling feeling, a bad vibe. Puzzled, they slowed down and wondered if the others felt something was wrong. No one could tell what was causing the eerie feeling they shared. Everything seemed completely nor-mal about the house. It was old but in decent shape — pleasant, quaint.

As night fell, they began to believe that the bad feeling was just in their heads. They went to bed — and that's when something really strange happened. Faintly they heard a disquieting *scritch-scritch-scritch* sound like nails running down a chalkboard a centimetre at a time. It came from inside the walls. It can be hard enough falling asleep in a new place, but this made it virtually impossible.

Soon after the first night, the family made an unsettling discovery. While brushing off the back step they found it was actually an inscribed tombstone, taken from a cemetery and repurposed for some unknown reason. Every time they stepped out back, it was like they were walking over the dead.

After this macabre revelation, the uneasy feeling of dread in the house worsened. The family felt tense every minute of every day. It seemed like they were being watched in each room. The kids jumped at every opportunity to sleep over at friends' houses, and even the parents found it difficult to get any rest.

Late one night, one of the boys woke to see a dark figure on the other side of his room. Half asleep, he assumed it was his brother. The boy drifted back to sleep as the figure crept toward his bed. When the boy woke in the morning, he found that his clothes had been thrown all about the room. When asked, his brother said he hadn't entered the room or touched the clothing.

That wasn't the last of the nighttime terrors. A little later, three members of the family stood frozen with fear as they watched an orb of red light appear near the staircase. It floated in the air as if it had a mind of its own before suddenly disappearing. Another night, a family friend was grabbed by invisible hands as soon as she passed through the front door. She heard an inhuman moan in her ear, but when she turned around no one was behind her. And shortly after, one of the boys fell asleep on a sofa in the small sitting room on the main floor. When he woke up he couldn't believe his eyes. There, in the middle of the floor, was a wide, dark grave, freshly dug and as wide as a giant mouth. He thought he must be dreaming, but the grave seemed so real he had to jump over it to escape the room. When he finally summoned the courage to show the others, the grave was gone.

This grave incident led the family to seek the council of a Roman Catholic priest. With holy water in hand, the old priest greeted the family and entered the house. He asked the family members to remain downstairs as he investigated the upper floors alone. The family waited, scared but hopeful that the priest would discover what was wrong with the house and cleanse it. They listened to his slow footsteps above. Before long the footsteps sped up as he moved deeper and higher into the house — he wasn't lingering in one place for long. Before completing his investigation of the third floor, the priest hurried back downstairs in a panic. The family asked him what had happened, what he had seen. He couldn't answer. With downcast eyes he shook his head and offered a dire warning: "I would advise you to leave." Without any further explanation, the priest fled from the property, never to return.

They didn't pack up and leave that night, but they didn't last much longer either. Just a few days later, whatever evil presence was haunting their house went absolutely haywire.

Everyone was asleep in their beds. Suddenly, a tumultuous racket erupted from the main floor. The parents and their children ran downstairs to see what was happening. It sounded like a truck had crashed through the front door and was driving straight through the house, but the truth was much more frightening.

A wooden hatch on the floor that led to a dirty crawl

space beneath the house was opening and closing repeatedly: *bang, bang, bang!* The unholy racket was relentless, sending everyone into hysterics. But nothing ever emerged from below. Perhaps that was for the best. As soon as the hatch stopped banging, their bedroom doors flew open and closed upstairs, and something pounded the walls all around them. When the sun finally rose in the morning, it felt like the night had lasted an eternity. But at least the racket had stopped. Shaken and exhausted, the family left. They didn't return.

The family had somehow managed to stay in the hellish house for four months, much longer than most would've lasted. An uncle who didn't believe in ghosts was happy to move in, but he only lived there for a month. He reached his limit when he woke up one morning and looked in the mirror to find angry red scratches running down his spine, all the way from his neck to his lower back.

The house was demolished in 1984 and the lot sat vacant for many years, as if no other building could take root. The land was eventually paved over to create a parking lot. But the family who lived there for four months can't forget what they lived through. One of the boys, now grown up, still suffers from nightmares. In his dreams he's forced back to the site of his childhood trauma. He stands outside the house and looks up. There, in one of the upper-floor windows, is a shadowy form looking back down at him.

The nightmare house — and its poltergeist — lives on in memory.

SENTENCED TO HANG

Victoria, British Columbia

In the mid to late 1800s, Victoria was full of rough-and-tumble men who had travelled to British Columbia seeking their fortunes in the Cariboo Gold Rush. Violence and bloodshed were commonplace. Sir Matthew Begbie presided over fifty-two murder cases, in twenty-seven of which the jury returned a guilty verdict. In those days, hanging was the standard death sentence for murderers, and Begbie soon became known far and wide as the Hanging Judge. Despite his reputation, Sir Begbie was tough but fair, and quite sympathetic toward minorities and the common man.

When the bodies of executed criminals were unclaimed by family, they were unceremoniously buried in unmarked graves. The Provincial Courthouse, now the Maritime

Museum, was built directly on top of this mass gravesite, and many people believe this history might explain the amount of paranormal activity that is reported there.

One day in June, Kristy Fallon, a museum employee, was in her office when she was suddenly overcome by an intense sobbing fit. As tears streamed down her face, she began to hyperventilate. She felt nauseated and her knees went weak. A co-worker had to rush her out of the building. It's believed one of the museum's ghosts, a crazed woman who haunts the courtroom, filled Kristy with negative energy. Many years ago the woman sat helplessly, watching her husband being tried and sentenced to death. She is now stuck in the courtroom to grieve for eternity.

Debra Doerksen and Dawn Kirkham, two mediums who have visited the museum on several occasions, have sensed up to forty-five ghosts. They say the museum is full of paranormal energy. When they visited one day with the crew of a local television show, each had a uniquely terrifying experience. Dawn saw a man who had been hanged in the 1880s. Although a length of rope was still tied around his neck, the man appeared confused and unaware that he was dead. He loudly proclaimed his innocence, forever pleading to be set free.

Debra, meanwhile, walked into a cramped and dingy room that was once used as the jail's holding cell and was immediately overcome by a painful tingling sensation in her head. The feeling was caused, she believed, by the spirit energy of a man who long ago repeatedly banged his head against the stone wall in an attempt to avoid his trial. It was an experience that left Debra shaken and in tears.

If you stand outside the Maritime Museum, the site of the old courthouse, and peer in through the front windows,

101.

Sir, Matthew Begbie c.f.

Canada

Sir Matthew Begbie

you might catch a glimpse of the Hanging Judge. People have reported seeing a tall, slender man with a long moustache and pointy beard silently gliding down the main staircase. Is he searching for another soul to sentence to hang or upset that his good name has been tarnished after his death? The jury is still out.

UNDER THE KNIFE

Calgary, Alberta

As the sun was beginning to set, a man entered the Riley Park Health Resource Centre, formerly the Grace Hospital. He was there to prepare for his back surgery that had been scheduled early the next morning. He hoped the procedure would bring him some relief, but the night that lay before him would be far from pain-free.

As soon as he stepped into his private room, he froze in his tracks and gasped. There was a woman sitting in the chair by the bed, coolly and silently staring at him. She had long, dark hair and wore a white dress. The man apologized and quickly stepped back into the hall, assuming he must have accidentally walked into the wrong room. But realization slowly washed over him. He hadn't walked into another patient's room. It was the woman in white who had made the mistake. He stepped back inside, but the chair was empty. The woman was gone — gone for the time being, that is.

Deeply unsettled, the man turned out the light and slipped beneath the hospital bedsheet. Maybe, he tried to convince himself, he had imagined the woman. Maybe the shadows had played a trick on him, some sort of ghostly optical illusion. He closed his eyes and, after tossing and turning, finally fell asleep.

His sleep, troubled as it was, didn't last long. He woke up when someone walked into his room. *The nurse*, the man thought, *it must be the nurse checking in on me.* Muffled footsteps crossed the room. Someone sat on the bed beside him, the bed squeaking softly under the weight. And then a hand gently touched his shoulder. The man rolled over to tell the nurse he was fine, but no one was there. This happened a few more times throughout the night, completely disrupting his sleep and fraying his nerves in the process.

The next morning, a nurse — a real, living nurse — wheeled his bed into a larger room and told him to hold tight for a little while. Six or seven other patients were wheeled into the same room and lined up in a row as the hospital staff prepared for the day.

"Have you seen my pen?" one of the nurses asked another. "I just had it."

"Maybe the ghost took it," the second nurse replied.

The row of eavesdropping patients laughed. But the man scheduled for back surgery remembered the woman in white sitting in his chair, the sounds of someone entering his room and sitting on his bed and the cold touch of phantom fingers upon his skin. He didn't join in the laughter.

Neither did the nurse who had suggested that the ghost might have been responsible for the missing pen. "No, seriously," she said without a trace of humour. Her tone was grave. She then told the patients — all of whom had abruptly ceased laughing — that the hospital is haunted. A woman wanders the halls, forever in search of her baby. The woman had died in childbirth and now things go missing all the time.

The man knew then, without a shadow of a doubt, that it was the grieving mother who had scared him so badly the night before. He was too shocked and upset to tell anyone what had happened to him.

The nurses who worked in the Grace Hospital noticed an odd pattern over the years. Time and again, women placed in the same room where the woman had died in labour experienced very difficult deliveries that lasted much longer than most. Many resulted in Caesarean sections, a surgical operation for delivering a child. The nurses came to believe that the ghost was trying to prevent other women from giving birth, perhaps in reaction to what had happened to her. Her ghost has been seen floating solemnly through the halls and has been heard opening windows and rattling the pipes. Occasionally, she gets into a little more trouble.

A guard was stationed in the hospital shortly after the maternity ward closed. That part of the building sat empty and unused before being repurposed, and the guard would often pass some time before the start of his shift in the room where the new mothers used to watch television. He'd been told the story of the ghost who couldn't bring herself to leave the scene of her death, but he chalked that up to the nurses telling tall tales and the other guards trying to spook him. He wasn't a believer, but he soon would be.

One night, the guard arrived to work early as usual. He went to the quiet, empty television room, pulled up a chair and watched an old episode of *Star Trek*. When the time came for him to begin work, he turned off the TV, returned his chair and left the room. As he walked through the halls, he started to feel a little weird. It seemed like someone was watching him, but he was certain he was alone. It was very dark and the red light of the exit signs cast a hellish glow around him.

As he continued on his way, he heard voices coming from a room at the end of the hall. The television room. He approached with caution, stepped inside and saw that someone had turned the TV back on. Someone had also pulled up the chair he had put away earlier. Casting nervous glances around the dark room, he radioed the other guard who was stationed at the desk and asked if anyone else was in the building.

"Just the engineer," the desk guard informed him. But the engineer was in the basement repairing something.

Trying to remain calm and hoping he didn't sound too panicked, the guard explained what had happened.

His colleague laughed. "Must be the ghosts having fun," he said.

Yeah, right, the guard thought. He wanted to laugh too, but he wasn't in a laughing mood. He turned off the TV, returned the chair for a second time and tried not to look over his shoulder as he left. He could still feel eyes on his back.

As he finished his patrol, the other guard radioed and told him to return to their security base immediately. He sounded anxious and scared. The guard hurried back and asked what the matter was. The desk guard pointed to the security board. A red light was flashing, indicating that someone had pushed a panic button in Operating Room 2, summoning security for help. The guard thought it must be some sort of joke, but his colleague said that no one else had keys to that area of the old maternity ward. Although he didn't want to, the guard had no other option but to go investigate who — or what — had pushed the button.

He slowly entered Operating Room 2, not sure what he'd find. Oddly, it was empty. But there on the wall, the security button was depressed. He pressed it and it popped back out with a click. His colleague radioed to tell him the light on the security board had gone out. The guard left, trying not to give the incident much thought. Better not to dwell on something he had no logical way to explain.

Not halfway back to the security base, his colleague radioed him again. Another light had turned on, this

Grace Hospital

time from Operating Room 1. The guard didn't hesitate. He sprinted to the room and barged inside, determined — perhaps a little frantic — to discover what was going on. Like the previous room, this one was also empty. Once again, the button had been pushed in, ruling out the possibility that a short circuit had triggered the alarms.

Not knowing what else to do and feeling at his wits' end, the guard stepped into the hallway. With Operating Room 1 behind him, Operating Room 2 to one side and the television room to the other, he raised his arms and pleaded with whomever might be listening and watching.

"Look," he said. "I know you might feel lonely, as all the babies and mothers are gone now. And I'm sorry that you feel this way. But I have a job to do. My job is to take care of this place and keep it safe. So I'm asking you, please don't keep calling us up here. We need to do our jobs. Thank you, and amen."

For whatever reason, the ghost obliged the guard. As long as he worked there, the security buttons were never pressed again. But that didn't stop the phantom eyes from trailing him as he walked his rounds, forever watching him through the night.

BURIED BELOW

Bonavista, Newfoundland and Labrador

It had been a long, tiring day and the old man wanted nothing more than to return home, crawl into bed and fall asleep. He drove through the night to his house near the Mockbeggar Plantation, a Provincial Historic Site in the small town of Bonavista, and pulled into his driveway. He killed the car's ignition and all was quiet and calm. Wearily, he stepped out of the car and approached his front gate. At the same moment that he opened it, someone opened the door of his enclosed porch.

The old man froze. He couldn't see anyone on the porch or in the yard. The only sounds were the crashing of ocean waves on the nearby shore and the insects buzzing in the grass around the house. He slowly closed the gate. The porch door swung shut as well.

After taking a moment to steel his nerve, the old man crossed the lawn and opened the porch door. The front door to his house followed suit. He closed the porch door behind him and, as before, the front door closed.

The old man opened the front door and stepped inside. Still unable to fathom what was happening, he watched as the kitchen door creaked open slowly.

And then he heard footsteps going up the stairs.

Knowing that his wife would be asleep in their bedroom, and fearful that she was in trouble, the man raced upstairs and barged into their room. He didn't pass anyone on the stairs or in the hall. His wife, alone in the bedroom, sat up in bed with a start. Before she could ask him what was wrong, he demanded to know if she had heard anyone climbing the stairs a moment ago.

"Yes," she said, a slight tremor creeping into her voice. "I thought it was you."

And then, loud at first but slowly fading, they heard the same footsteps walking back down the stairs. This bizarre and unnerving phenomenon occurred on several more occasions.

One day in the spring, the old man was doing some renovations and digging on his property when his shovel hit something solid, something the man never would have expected to discover. Buried deep beneath his house's foundation was a casket. He and his wife had been living for years above a dead body. Once the casket was removed, his doors stopped opening and closing on their own and the couple never heard phantom footsteps going up and down their stairs again.

In any other town, finding a casket buried under your house would be completely unusual, but Bonavista is not any other town. When a canal was dug in the 1920s, the construction crew discovered a number of unmarked coffins buried in the mud. More coffins were unearthed during the construction of a bridge in 1946. The caskets were pried open and the remains of men, women and children were found inside. They were dressed in European-style clothing, and the wood of the coffins was not native to Newfoundland. Experts believe the caskets predate 1725, the year the first cemetery was built in Bonavista.

Where did the coffins come from? Why were they buried in Bonavista? And who were the people left to rot beneath the homes that would later be built above them? Some believe the deceased must have been early French settlers, since many men came from France to fish the Newfoundland coast. Others discredit this theory because French fishermen did not bring their wives or children to Canada. It remains one of the great mysteries of Canada's past, and it's a decidedly macabre mystery to boot.

Whoever they were and however they ended up in their final resting place, the spirits of the departed have not gone quietly into the night. It's not uncommon for people to hear the lilting voices of men and women singing in a foreign language, carried by the midnight wind from the burial grounds where the coffins were discovered.

THE SPIRIT OF THE CATHEDRAL

Quebec City, Quebec

Loud, triumphant music poured from the Cathedral of the Holy Trinity's celebrated organ, filling the building from its pews to its domed ceiling. There was only one man in the church, the organist, and he was concentrating so hard as he practised his music that he didn't hear the sound of approaching footsteps. When he did hear someone approaching, he stopped playing and spun around — the echoes of his music faded to silence. He picked up his sheet music, stood up and peered around the church. Although he could still hear the footsteps getting closer, closer, closer, he couldn't see a soul.

The footsteps grew louder and suddenly stopped to the organist's left. Then the source of the disturbance materialized before his eyes. A woman wearing an old-fashioned dress and hat appeared in front of one of the church's stained-glass windows. Cold sweat trickled into the man's eyes and he could barely breathe. Before he could do anything, the woman disappeared.

A moment later the organ began blaring, an angry sound that reverberated through the air. The organist dropped his sheet music in terror and, as he fled from his instrument and the phantom that was playing it, the blaring turned into a melodic tune not unlike the one the organist had been playing only a minute or two before.

Many have seen the spirit of the cathedral. She has frightened and disturbed organists and churchgoers alike with the sound of her hollow footfalls and tearful moans. Who she is — or rather, was — is a bit of a mystery, but it's widely believed that she is one of two women who have deadly ties to the cathedral's early days.

The Cathedral of the Holy Trinity, the first Anglican Cathedral to be built outside the British Isles, was constructed shortly before a cholera epidemic swept through Quebec City. In June of 1832 a few feverish passengers disembarked a ship that had travelled from Ireland to Quebec, and the first known fatality occurred soon after. Within a few short days, cholera had spread to Montreal and into Upper Canada. Suddenly hundreds were dying every day. Doctors were overwhelmed with patients, and officials went to extreme, desperate measures to try to stop the disease from spreading further. Officers fired cannons and the Sanitary Office burned tar in an attempt to cleanse the air.

Iris Dillon lived near the church and in great fear. As scared as she was of the disease that was killing her neighbours and friends, she was even more afraid that she would somehow end up buried alive. Iris suffered from

Organ of the Cathedral of the Holy Trinity

narcolepsy, a neurological disorder that causes people to fall into deep slumbers from which they cannot be roused. Tragically, Iris's greatest fear came true. A neighbour found her in a narcoleptic state and, when he could not wake her, thought she was dead and alerted the authorities. During the epidemic, bodies were dealt with swiftly without prayer or ceremony, and it's believed Iris was buried alive in the church's cemetery. During construction fifty years later, a workman dug up human remains believed to belong to Iris Dillon, who might be the ghost of the cathedral.

The second possibility is a young woman who — approximately thirty years after the cholera epidemic — gave birth to a baby out of wedlock. This was gravely frowned upon in the 1860s, and both the woman and her newborn became social outcasts. Unable to provide for her child and convinced she had no other options, the woman made a horrible decision. Late one night she suffocated her baby with a pillow, crept into the cathedral's basement and buried the small body in the ground beside the remains of entombed bishops. It's rumoured that there's a small, unmarked grave in the cathedral's basement directly beneath the position of the organ.

Some organists have reported that placing toys on the grave has allowed them to practise without the ghostly woman disturbing them. It's believed the young mother, guilt-ridden over her horrific actions, haunts the church seeking forgiveness for the crime she committed more than 150 years ago.

Whether the ghost is a woman who was buried alive or a woman who killed her own child, she's unable to find solace and move on. The cathedral is one of Ghost Tours of Quebec's main stops, and at least two of the leaders have encountered the ghost on separate occasions.

Laurie Thatcher was speaking to a group one night when she saw the ghost standing on the second floor balcony near the organ. Sweat poured down Laurie's face and her heart pounded against her ribcage. She wanted out of the church immediately.

Another night, a different guide had an odd sensation that she was being watched from behind while she spoke to a group. Shaking the feeling off, she retrieved her lantern — which she had set on a table behind her — and noticed that not only had the light gone out, but the candle had disappeared entirely. Confused and a little shaken, the guide wondered aloud what had happened to the candle. A man on the tour then told her he had seen a shadowy figure standing near the lantern as she spoke.

It seems nothing will bring the spirit any peace, for she still haunts the cathedral today, playing the organ and terrifying people.

ARMY OF THE DEAD

Louisbourg, Nova Scotia

The mid-afternoon sun sparkled across the water of Louisbourg Harbour and warmed the backs of the assembled tourists, giving the tour leader no reason to expect anything sinister lay in wait beyond the chapel door.

Beckoning the group to follow her as she recounted historical tales of what life was like in the Fortress of Louisbourg during the 1700s, the guide opened the door and stepped inside. She had expected the chapel to be empty. It wasn't. A man in period clothing was kneeling at the altar, weeping loudly and shouting in French.

That's odd, thought the guide. There weren't supposed to be any re-enactors, or "animators," in the church. Thanks to restoration efforts by Parks Canada and the Fortress Louisbourg Association, the fortress has been rebuilt by archaeologists and the streets are filled during the summer months with animators, people portraying the rich and the poor, the old and the young, exactly as people lived in 1744. But that church, at that time of day, was supposed to be empty.

The guide did her best to pretend the crying man was a planned part of the tour and carried on spinning tales of the founding of the fortress in 1713 by the French, of its heyday as a thriving fishing settlement and of its eventual destruction in the 1760s at the hands of the British. But the man continued cursing and crying with equal amounts of anger and sorrow, and the guide had to shout to be heard over the racket. Despite her best efforts to remain calm, she lost her train of thought and finally snapped.

She turned to the man at the altar and shouted at him, demanding to know what, exactly, he was supposed to be re-enacting.

The tour guide didn't receive a response. But her group of tourists looked at one another in shock and asked each other why their guide was shouting at an empty altar. The guide was the only person who could see and hear him.

The Fortress of Louisbourg is haunted by an army of the dead, the spirits of soldiers and settlers who lived there long ago. These ghosts, like the man shouting in French in the chapel, are regularly mistaken for the living, breathing animators who recreate history for the visitors of this National Historic Site.

In October, guides lead nighttime tours through the streets of the fortress. It's so large that it includes three authentic eighteenth-century restaurants where stew simmers over open flames, a parlour where women lead dancing demonstrations, the King's Bakery with its delectable aroma of fresh-baked bread and army barracks where the ground shakes from the firing of the fortress cannon. It's so real, Fortress staff say, it seems *surreal*. Surreal is a very apt choice of word.

On cold autumn nights, the only light comes from the moon, candles lit in windows and lanterns carried by the guides. They share some of the more unsettling and morbid stories that have been reported over the years.

At the end of a long, busy night, a guide noticed a candle still burning in one of the barracks's windows. She entered the building to blow out the candle but was surprised to find a soldier sitting beside the flickering light. Startled, she breathlessly said, "You'd better hurry up and get changed. The bus is about to leave." She then blew out the candle and quickly left. The man didn't answer or follow her out.

Dark study at the Fortress of Louisbourg

After exiting the barracks, she told the bus driver to wait for the final animator. Everyone on the bus asked her who she was talking about. "There's still a soldier up there getting changed," she replied, the first hints of unease creeping into her voice. "I just spoke to him." The military supervisor looked at her gravely and informed her everyone was already on the bus. The last person had left the barracks ten minutes ago. There was no one — no one living — inside the barracks.

Sometimes the animators spend the entire weekend inside the fortress to fully submerge themselves into the lives of those who lived there during the 1700s. During one such encampment, an animator who was portraying a member of the French militia was sleeping in the Chevalier house. In the middle of the night she awoke to see three men in British uniform and one First Nations man standing in the large room where others were also sleeping. She assumed the four strangers were fellow animators who had entered the building to find a friend and she rolled over and let herself drift back to sleep. But in the morning, when she described the four men and asked who they were, the British animators shared wide-eyed looks and informed her that they didn't have any uniforms in the style she had seen, nor was there a First Nations man with them. Furthermore, they all insisted that no one in their party had visited the Chevalier house during the night.

Perhaps the creepiest house on the property is the Duhaget home. Captain Duhaget built the house for his wife and the children they hoped to fill it with. Unfortunately, they were unable to conceive a baby, and the captain fell into poor health and died, leaving his wife a widow in the empty home. It's believed the captain couldn't bear the thought of his wife being left alone without children for company, so he took it upon himself to return after death.

When the Duhaget house was being updated for modern-day visitors, the exhibit designer was alone when he saw a uniformed man walk past the stairwell. The stranger's costume was remarkably realistic, particularly his coat. When the exhibit designer later visited the costume department, he told them how impressed he was with the uniforms they had created. Unable to contain her puzzlement, the costume designer informed the man that they did not have any coats in their collection to match his description, and the animators hadn't arrived at the fortress yet. The man could think of only one explanation: he had seen the ghost of Duhaget, and that's why the coat had looked so authentic.

As chilling as the realization that he had seen a ghost was for the poor exhibit designer, perhaps he'd find comfort in the knowledge that Captain Duhaget's ghost seems to be more concerned with protecting guests in his home than terrifying them. One day, when a guide was descending the back stairs, she tripped on the carpet and fell. She would have been seriously injured if not for an invisible hand that reached out of thin air and grabbed her by the shoulder, holding her upright and preventing her from tumbling down to what might have been an early grave.

So real, it's surreal, indeed. Set foot in the Fortress of Louisbourg and you might find yourself marching with the army of the dead.

THE MYSTERY OF BINSTEAD HOUSE

Charlottetown, Prince Edward Island

It was in 1884 that Georgina Mary Pennée found herself in the company of Alfred, Lord Tennyson, the English Poet Laureate. She was visiting her ailing brother who lived in Weston Manor on the Isle of Wight, England, and Lord Tennyson was a neighbour and friend. They sat beside the fire and talked late into the night when Georgina shared a story from her past. A dark, disturbing story, one she hadn't shared widely. It was a ghost story, but it wasn't one she had heard and it most certainly wasn't fictional. It was a story she had lived through while she lived on Prince Edward Island.

Overlooking the Hillsborough River and surrounded by tall, mature trees, the Binstead House sits alone on a large piece of property in Charlottetown, Prince Edward Island.

Built in 1833 by John Levitt, Esq., the large home is as white as a ghost and pockmarked by shuttered windows. It was formally recognized as a Historic Place in 1999. It's not common for private residences to receive historic designations for being haunted, but that's how Binstead House rose to infamy.

Georgina was a respectable English woman and the daughter of William Ward, a Director of the Bank of England and one of the era's most celebrated cricket players. Georgina married Arthur Pennée in 1850 and, six years later, they moved into Binstead House.

It was a large home that had chambers for the men hired to farm the estate's fields, making it an abode that was both beautiful and profitable. But the perfect, peaceful facade didn't last long. A mere ten days after the Pennées moved in, strange things started happening.

Late at night, after the last candle had been snuffed and the smell of smoke hung in the air, hair-raising noises wracked the house. It was a rumbling sound that seemed to shake the entire building. Georgina compared it to the noise "produced by dragging a heavy body, which one so often hears in ghost stories." This continued each night for several weeks and was heard in all areas of the house. If only the rumbling was the worst sound the Pennées would hear in their home. Unfortunately, it was not.

As winter turned to spring, the rumbling was accompanied by the shrieks and sobs of an unseen person. The uproar always seemed to start outside, at the base of a tree that stood beside the dining room window. The screams then entered the house and flew from room to room, growing louder and louder, as if some phantom were being chased around the property. Sometimes Georgina heard moaning and muffled words, but the voice was always disembodied. It wasn't until February of 1857 that the source of the phantom voice made itself seen.

Two island women, a Mrs. M. and a Miss C., visited the Pennées as overnight guests. They were set up in a rarely used spare bedroom on the second floor and, after supper and some socializing, retired for the night. The two women slipped into the bed and left the fire burning to keep them warm as they slept. Outside the bedroom window, the gnarled branches of the tree from which the ghostly wails always started reached for the glass pane but fell a little short.

At two o'clock in the morning, Mrs. M. was suddenly awoken by a white light that filled the room. She knew immediately that it couldn't be the fire — it was far too bright. She glanced about the room and saw, standing beside the fireplace, a woman in a checkered shawl with her back to the bed. The light was somehow, inexplicably, flowing straight out of the woman. But Mrs. M. could see that the woman held, in her left arm, a young baby.

Confused and growing a little fearful, Mrs. M. shook Miss C. to awaken her. Suddenly, the woman with the baby spun around and faced them. Her young face was filled with anxiety. Miss C. was convinced their room had been invaded by a ghost. She screamed and pulled the bedsheet over her head and Mrs. M's. They remained covered for the remainder of the night, not daring to peek out from beneath the sheet for fear of what they might see.

The ghost reappeared in the same room the following spring, and this time Georgina witnessed it herself. Her daughter was sick and had moved into the guest room, so Georgina decided to spend the night by her side to keep an eye on her. A little past midnight Georgina got up to fetch some medicine when her daughter noticed a bright light shining under the door from the hall. Believing the light meant her husband was outside, Georgina opened the door quickly and was completely shocked when she found herself face to face with a young woman. The woman held a baby in her left arm and wore a checkered shawl tied across her chest. Georgina knew immediately that this was the same woman her guests had seen before.

The two women — one living, one dead — stared silently at each other, neither able to move or find her voice. Light radiated out of the dead woman and her baby in waves. She looked at Georgina with an agonized stare and then, without so much as a single word, she turned, took a few steps away and disappeared straight through a wall.

After a brief trip home to England, Georgina returned to discover that the creature, as her family and their farm-hands had taken to calling the ghost, had been "carrying on," and that her nightly screams had intensified. A young boy named Harry, who worked on the farm, admitted that the ghost had appeared in his room many times. He refused to share many details of the nighttime visits, but he did reveal that he had often woken from fretful sleeps to see the woman standing at the foot of his bed. Harry refused to allow anyone else to share his room and insisted on locking himself in every night. It was unclear whether Harry hoped to keep the ghost out to protect himself . . . or in to protect the others.

The Pennées moved out of Binstead in 1861 and reset-tled in Quebec. But in 1877 Georgina returned to PEI for several months. One day Father Boudreault, the parish priest, approached her with a letter in his hand, asking if she could shed any light on its contents. It was written by Mrs. Carey, who was the current owner of Binstead. In it Mrs. Carey pleaded with the priest to visit her home to dispel the ghost of a woman with a baby in her arms, a ghost that had troubled her since she'd moved in.

Georgina decided to launch a personal investigation to find the root of the haunting. She discovered that the house was once owned by a farmer named Braddock, who she described as "a man of low tastes and immoral habits." Two sisters, both of whom had baby boys, had worked for Braddock.

Digging a little deeper, a difficult task since respectable people had avoided Braddock due to his character, Georgina learned that one of the sisters had disappeared with one of the babies. But what exactly happened to her was a mystery lost to time. Before the remaining baby turned two, Braddock sold the house and left the area. The remaining sister returned to her parents' house and gave them the baby. It wasn't her baby, she told them, but her sister's. Her own baby, she said sadly, had died. She revealed nothing further and refused to answer their distraught questions, then ran away to America and never returned.

The surviving boy's name was Harry. He was, Georgina realized in shock, the same Harry whom she had hired as a farmhand years later. The same Harry who had been visited by the ghost of a woman holding a baby in her arms. The same Harry who had locked the door and refused to speak on the matter any further.

It's not a stretch to assume that the ghost is Harry's mother, and the baby in her arms his cousin. But puzzling questions remain. How did they die? Did Braddock play a part in their deaths? Why did the sound of the woman's midnight screams always start at the base of the tree? Did the tree have something to do with their deaths, perhaps, or were they buried in the earth at its base?

Georgina found the courage to return to Binstead one final time in 1888. The first thing she noticed was that the ominous tree had been cut down. She then spoke with Mrs. Carey, the woman who had written the letter to the parish priest, and her husband. They revealed that no one had slept in the guest room since they'd occupied the house. Georgina asked if she could spend one night in the room with the ghost, but Mrs. Carey flatly refused. The priest had blessed the house and the matter was closed. Mrs. Carey said no more.

With a little further prodding, Mr. Carey let slip that the ghost had been seen twice since the priest's visit, once near the front entrance and again in an upstairs window. But after a sharp look from his wife, Mr. Carey corrected himself, emphasizing that the ghost had only *allegedly* been seen, as if that somehow made the situation more palatable.

Thus ended Georgina's investigation into the haunting of the Binstead House. Lord Tennyson, riveted by the ghastly tale, requested that Georgina write the story down, and Georgina obliged. A few years later, Georgina's story was discovered by the English Society for Psychical Research, and soon after it became known around the world. It remains one of the most mysterious unsolved ghost cases ever to have occurred in PEI.

SPIRITS OF THE SLIDE

Crowsnest Pass, Alberta

Tours of the Turtle Mountain coal mines, which are nestled in the scenic Municipality of Crowsnest Pass, are offered every fall. Some visitors come for the history, others come for a glimpse into a restricted area and still others come for the claustrophobic thrill of being completely immersed in darkness. It's all in a day's work for the tour guides, but one of them, oddly, has heard the chirping of canaries deep in the bowels of the earth.

Canaries used to be taken into mines to warn the men of carbon monoxide poisoning. If the canaries died, an alarm was sounded and the miners would rush out into the clean air. There are no longer canaries in Turtle Mountain's mines, but the guide is still certain she hears their song calling through the darkness.

It was a separate event that assured her that even when she is alone in the mine, she's never *truly* alone. One night as she prepared for the next tour group, the guide heard the mine shaft door open, followed by voices and the sound of approaching feet. She saw no people, no lanterns, and yet the sound of people came closer and closer. When the sound of the group was practically on top of her, she had a sickening realization. A class of school children was scheduled for the next tour, but the voices in the darkness belonged to grown men. Suddenly the door opened again and the sounds of the men abruptly stopped. She saw lanterns approaching, held in the small hands of children.

When she later told some of the other guides what she had heard, she asked who the first group of men to enter the mine had been. Her companions looked at her like she was crazy. No one else had entered the mine before the children. She had been completely alone.

During the 1800s, the First Nations people of southern Alberta avoided Turtle Mountain. They called it the "mountain that moves." Little did the citizens of the community of Frank know that the mountain that towered more than 2,100 metres above them would indeed move. And it would completely eradicate nearly everything that stood in its path.

At 4:10 a.m. on April 29, 1903, 82 million tonnes of limestone broke free from the mountain and roared down its slope into Crowsnest Pass. The limestone broke apart into colossal boulders that destroyed 75 percent of Frank, buried the entrance to the mine, ploughed across the valley and even climbed approximately 150 metres up a neighbouring mountain. Of the town's six hundred inhabitants, more than seventy people lost their lives. It was, and still is to this day, Canada's biggest and deadliest rock slide.

Debris field from the landslide that destroyed Frank, Alberta

Today, the rocks remain where they fell, forming a giant graveyard above the land where many of the bodies could not be retrieved from the rubble. Monica Field, who works for the Frank Slide Interpretive Centre, is aware of the ghost stories that have sprouted from the area's history. She calls it, "an area of such concentrated suffering." How could it not be home to a spectre or two?

Children who live nearby make sport of climbing the

massive boulders left behind by the slide. But no one, if they're being honest, ever feels quite right in the area. They report an uneasy, sickening feeling of being watched at all times. Hikers have crested hills only to see the silhouettes of miners staring down on them from farther up the mountain. And it's said that an archaeologist was accosted by the ghost of a miner wielding a pickaxe, warning the archaeologist to leave. He did, and quickly.

The eerie feeling that permeates the air might be caused by the fact that so many lives were lost in such a short period of time. The rock slide was a tragedy that was over in a minute and a half, but it appears as if some of its victims now remain tied to this world for an eternity.

SPOOKY HOLLOW

Norfolk County, Ontario

Picture yourself driving through Normandale, a small, sleepy town not unlike the countless others that dot Canada's vast countryside. Your car drives up a steep hill, past harvested fields and the Gothic-style gates of a small cemetery. At the top of the hill you see a sign and must make a choice: turn right and continue on your way, or continue straight ahead toward Spooky Hollow.

Ghostly legends and lore abound in Spooky Hollow, which isn't surprising given its creepy name, which could have come straight out of a fairy tale — one of the dark, scary ones where things don't necessarily end happily ever after.

Once long ago, during an unusually warm day in early fall, a young Normandale couple named Peter and Janet spent a relaxing day at the beach not too far from their hometown. As the sun began to dip behind the silhouetted pine trees on the horizon, they packed Peter's car and started for home. Night fell upon them as they drove along the twisty country roads, the car's headlights reflecting off animal eyes in the woods. It was a humid night and they drove with the windows down, enjoying the wind and fresh air. Long, wispy tendrils of fog crept out from between the trees, but Peter didn't let that bother him. Not wanting the day to end, he decided he'd take the scenic route home. He turned off the paved highway, onto the gravel road that snaked through the heart of Spooky Hollow.

The fog thickened as the forest became denser, darker. It was hard to see more than a few feet in front of the car, and Peter had to slow to a crawl. Suddenly, the car's engine backfired and the vehicle jumped. The couple cried out in shock. Peter pushed down on the gas pedal, but instead of accelerating, the car slowly came to a stop. Peter tried to restart it, but nothing happened. The engine was dead. They looked under the hood but had no idea how to fix the car. So Peter volunteered to walk to the nearest farmhouse — there had to be one nearby, although he couldn't remember passing one in a long, long time — and ask to use their phone to call a tow truck. He told Janet to stay in the car, lock the doors and stay warm under a blanket. He'd return soon.

He didn't. An hour passed, then two, then three, but still there was no sign of him. Janet grew increasingly scared and concerned. He should have been back long ago. Eventually Janet grew so tired that even her fear couldn't keep her awake, and she slipped into a troubled sleep.

She didn't sleep for long. A loud thump rocked the hood of the car and startled her awake. Her heart jumped into her throat and she peered out into the dark fog but could see nothing.

"Peter?" she called out uncertainly, hoping her boyfriend had returned.

A second bang shook the car, the only response to her call. She yelled and pulled the blanket up to her chin, frozen with fear. Fortunately, Peter soon returned with help, but when Janet told him what had happened and he investigated the area, he found no trace or sign that anyone had been near the car. The only explanation the couple could fathom was that the car had been struck twice by one of the ghosts that gave Spooky Hollow its name.

Some say a travelling salesman once sought refuge in a stranger's home where he met a grisly end. A wicked storm made it impossible for his horse to carry on any further and he knocked on the door of the first house he came upon. Luckily, he thought, the owner welcomed him in. But he turned out to be anything but lucky. He was murdered and dismembered in the middle of the night, and the sky above was choked for days with black smoke that spewed from the house's chimney. Those who passed by noticed that a pungent, repulsive smell accompanied the smoke, giving rise to the belief that the salesman's body was burned in the fireplace to destroy evidence of the murder.

Others believe a gang of criminals who illegally transported alcohol from Canada to the United States in the 1920s, during Prohibition, haunt the woods. One day they were ambushed and gunned down by the local law enforcement, soaking the dirt with their blood and trapping their spirits in the forest.

But the story that has gained the most notoriety involves a small hotel that once sheltered travellers more than one hundred years ago. The hotel caught fire one night and was reduced to cinders and ash. Not everyone was able to escape. Someone died in the blaze. And as you might imagine, the victim's ghost is none too fond of fire.

Only the bravest human beings can tell you if this is true, but if you want to experience the scare of a lifetime you should venture into Spooky Hollow on Halloween. Find a secluded clearing in the woods — anywhere will do. Wait for night to fall. When the clock strikes midnight, light a match and listen closely. As the flame burns down you'll hear agonizing screams in the distance, as pain-ridden and real as the day the victim died in the fire.

EPILOGUE

Still don't believe in ghosts? Then maybe you should spend a night — alone — in a haunted house. That's what I decided to do while writing some of the stories you hold in your hands. Throughout my research I was astounded by the credibility of the ghost stories I unearthed, by the sheer number of eyewitness accounts that lined up with one another, by the ability of the tales to get under my skin and send me running around my darkened home turning on every single light.

I had never seen a ghost myself. Don't ask me why (morbid curiosity, most likely), but I wanted to — needed to — change that.

And so I drove to the picturesque town of Niagara-on-the-Lake and checked into The Olde Angel Inn. You know an inn is old when it spells the word with an E. In fact, it's the oldest inn in Ontario, incorporated in 1789. It burned down (and was later rebuilt) after the War of 1812. It's a beautiful building that has sheltered many famous guests over the years, including the first Lieutenant-Governor of Upper Canada, John Graves Simcoe; explorer Alexander Mackenzie; and Queen Victoria's father, Prince Edward. In short, it's seen a lot of history, and some of that history has been bloody.

Naturally, The Olde Angel Inn has a resident ghost.

During a secret rendezvous at the inn with his sweetheart, Captain Colin Swayze of the British Army hid in the cellar when he received word that American soldiers had invaded the town. He slipped into a barrel and hoped he'd go undetected. He didn't. The Americans stormed the inn, thundered down the cellar steps and stabbed each of the barrels with their bayonets. Captain Swayze spent his final living moments alone and afraid as he watched the blood drain from his body.

Shortly after the captain's death, people began witnessing odd things, and reports of paranormal activity continue to this day. Items fly off shelves. Footsteps plod down empty halls. A man in an old-fashioned military uniform walks through rooms in the middle of the night without pausing to open doors.

After interviewing staff and being guided into the cramped cellar to see the exact spot where Captain Swayze was killed, I spent a night in the General's Quarters, the Angel's most haunted bedroom. I locked myself in (little good that would do), left the lights on and pulled the bedsheet up to my chin.

Unexplained noises filled the room throughout the night. Out of the corner of my eye I saw countless shadows moving about. A curtain rustled as if someone hid behind it. My room key, dangling over the edge of a small table in the corner of the room where most of the paranormal activity has been witnessed, swayed from side to side on its own — I checked for a draft or an open window but the air around the key was dead still. A toy rabbit my daughter had lent me rested on the floor facing my bed as I finally fell into a restless sleep. When I woke up, the rabbit was in the exact same spot . . . but had turned 180 degrees to face the wall.

I'm not exaggerating when I say I've never been so creeped out in my life. The goosebumps on my arms could've been used to sand wood.

Don't believe me? I had a feeling you might say that.

So I decided to record the entire night with my camcorder. You can watch the video of my night alone in the haunted Olde Angel Inn on Scholastic Canada's website at www. scholastic.ca/hauntedcanada.

But before you visit the website and press play, make sure the lights are on. Grab a friend or sibling for safety in numbers. Make sure there's nothing under the bed or in the deepest corners of your closet, just in case.

And beware toy rabbits.

PHOTO CREDITS

Joel A. Sutherland is an author and librarian. He is the author of several books in the Haunted Canada series, as well as *Be a Writing Superstar, Summer's End* and Haunted, a series of middle-grade horror novels. His short fiction has appeared in many anthologies and magazines, alongside the likes of Stephen King and Neil Gaiman. He has been a juror for the John Spray Mystery Award and the Monica Hughes Award for Science Fiction and Fantasy.

He appeared as "The Barbarian Librarian" on the Canadian edition of the hit television show *Wipeout,* making it all the way to the third round and proving that librarians can be just as tough and crazy as anyone else.

Joel lives with his family in southeastern Ontario, where he is always on the lookout for ghosts.

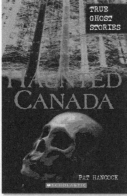

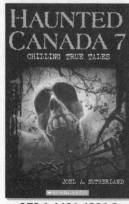